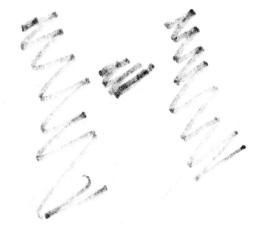

The Goal
of the Lord's
Recovery—
to Bring Forth
the One
New Man

The Holy Word for Morning Revival

Witness Lee

Living Stream Ministry
Anaheim, CA • www.lsm.org

First Edition, March 2018.

ISBN 978-0-7363-9132-0

Published by

Living Stream Ministry
2431 W. La Palma Ave., Anaheim, CA 92801 U.S.A.
P. O. Box 2121, Anaheim, CA 92814 U.S.A.

Printed in the United States of America

18 19 20 / 4 3 2 1

2018 International Chinese-speaking Conference

THE GOAL OF THE LORD'S RECOVERY—
TO BRING FORTH THE ONE NEW MAN

Contents

Preface

1. This book is intended as an aid to believers in developing a daily time of morning revival with the Lord in His word. At the same time, it provides a limited review of the International Chinese-speaking Conference held in Taipei, Taiwan, February 16-18, 2018. The subject of the conference was "The Goal of the Lord's Recovery—to Bring Forth the One New Man." Through intimate contact with the Lord in His word, the believers can be constituted with life and truth and thereby equipped to prophesy in the meetings of the church unto the building up of the Body of Christ.

2. The book is divided into weeks. One conference message is covered per week. Each week presents first the message outline, followed by six daily portions, a hymn, and then some space for writing. The message outline has been divided into days, corresponding to the six daily portions. Each daily portion covers certain points and begins with a section entitled "Morning Nourishment." This section contains selected verses and a short reading that can provide rich spiritual nourishment through intimate fellowship with the Lord. The "Morning Nourishment" is followed by a section entitled "Today's Reading," a longer portion of ministry related to the day's main points. Each day's portion concludes with a short list of references for further reading and some space for the saints to make notes concerning their spiritual inspiration, enlightenment, and enjoyment to serve as a reminder of what they have received of the Lord that day.

3. The space provided at the end of each week is for composing a short prophecy. This prophecy can be composed by considering all of our daily notes, the "harvest" of our inspirations during the week, and preparing a main point with some sub-points to be spoken in the church meetings for the organic building up of the Body of Christ.

4. Following the last week in this volume, we have provided reading schedules for both the Old and New Testaments in

the Recovery Version with footnotes. These schedules are arranged so that one can read through both the Old and New Testaments of the Recovery Version with footnotes in two years.

5. As a practical aid to the saints' feeding on the Word throughout the day, we have provided verse cards at the end of the volume, which correspond to each day's Scripture reading. These may be cut out and carried along as a source of spiritual enlightenment and nourishment in the saints' daily lives.

6. The content of this book is taken primarily from the conference message outlines, the text and footnotes of the Recovery Version of the Bible, selections from the writings of Witness Lee and Watchman Nee, and *Hymns,* all of which are published by Living Stream Ministry.

7. The conference message outlines were compiled by Living Stream Ministry from the writings of Witness Lee and Watchman Nee. The outlines, footnotes, and cross-references in the Recovery Version of the Bible are by Witness Lee. Unless otherwise noted, the references cited in this publication are by Witness Lee.

8. For the sake of space, references to *The Collected Works of Watchman Nee* and *The Collected Works of Witness Lee* are abbreviated to *CWWN* and *CWWL,* respectively.

International Chinese-speaking Conference
(February 16-18, 2018)

General Subject:

The Goal of the Lord's Recovery—
to Bring Forth the One New Man

Banners:

The goal of the Lord's recovery
is to bring forth the one new man—
a corporate, universal man—
for the fulfillment of God's eternal purpose.

The key to the practical existence
of the one new man—
to putting off the old man
and putting on the new man—
is in being renewed in the spirit of our mind.

We need to take Christ as our person,
grow up into Christ in all things,
and learn Christ as the reality is in Jesus
for the corporate living of the one new man.

As we are ruled by the peace of Christ
and inhabited by the word of Christ
through persevering in prayer,
He permeates and replaces us with Himself
until all our natural distinctions
have been eliminated,
and we become the new man in reality.

Our Urgent Need to See the Vision
of the Church as the One New Man

Scripture Reading: Prov. 29:18a; Acts 26:19; Eph. 2:15-16; 4:24; Col. 3:10-11

Day 1

Warren

I. **In the last days of this age, before the Lord is able to return, we must see the vision of the one Body and the one new man (1 Cor. 12:12; Eph. 2:15; 4:4, 24):**

   A. In the Bible *vision* denotes an extraordinary scene; it refers to a special kind of seeing—a glorious, inward seeing—and to the spiritual scenery we see from God (Prov. 29:18a; Acts 26:19; Ezek. 1:1; Dan. 7:1, 9-10, 13-14):

   1. The heavenly vision governs us, restricts us, controls us, directs us, preserves us, revolutionizes us, keeps us in the genuine oneness, and gives us the boldness to go on (Prov. 29:18a).

   2. Under the heavenly vision we are directed toward God's destination, and our life is controlled according to God's economy (Phil. 3:13-14; 1 Tim. 1:4).

Day 2

Harolds

   B. Ultimately, the Bible speaks of the church as the one new man (Matt. 16:18; Eph. 1:22-23; 2:15; 4:24; Col. 3:10-11):

   1. As the one new man, the church is a corporate person and needs Christ not only as its life but also as its person (Eph. 3:17a; 4:24; Col. 3:4, 10).

   2. For the practical existence of the one new man, we all need to take Christ as our person (Eph. 3:17a).

II. **The church is the one new man to accomplish God's eternal purpose (1:9, 11; 3:11; Rom. 8:28; Eph. 2:15-16; 4:22-24):**

   A. God's intention in His creation of man was to have a corporate man to express Him and to represent Him (Gen. 1:26):

　　1. God's creation of man in Genesis 1 is a picture of the one new man in God's new creation; this means that the old creation is a figure, a type, of the new creation (Eph. 2:15; 4:24).

Day 3

Korean

　　2. God created man in His own image and then gave man His dominion (Gen. 1:26).

　　3. Eventually, the church as the one new man is the corporate man in God's intention (Col. 3:10).

　B. The Bible reveals that the one new man is a corporate, universal man (Eph. 2:15; 4:24):

　　1. We, the believers in Christ, are all one with Christ to be the new man; thus, we all are parts, components, of the corporate one new man (Col. 3:10-11).

　　2. The one new man is a corporate God-man, the aggregate of all the God-men (Eph. 2:15; 4:24).

III. The one new man was created through Christ's death on the cross (2:15-16):

　A. The one new man was created by Christ with two kinds of materials—the redeemed created man and the divine element; on the cross Christ put these two elements together to produce a new man (v. 15).

Day 4

Ritero's

　B. Apart from being in Christ, we could not have been created into one new man, because in ourselves we do not have the divine essence, which is the element of the one new man (v. 15):

　　1. Only in the divine essence and with the divine essence were we created into the one new man; it is possible to have this essence only in Christ.

　　2. In the one new man Christ is all because He is the essence with which the new man was created; therefore, the one new man is Christ (Col. 3:10-11).

IV. The one new man is Christ constituted into us (vv. 10-11):

    A. The Christ who indwells us is the constituent of the one new man (1:27; 3:11).

    B. As we experience and enjoy the all-inclusive Christ, He is constituted into us, and we become the one new man (1:12-13; 3:10).

    C. In the one new man Christ is all the members and is in all the members (v. 11).

    D. The only way that Christ can be all and in all in the one new man is for Him to be constituted into us (Gal. 4:19; Eph. 3:17a).

Day 5

V. The goal of the Lord's recovery is to bring forth the one new man (2:15; 4:22-24; Col. 3:10-11):

    A. What the Lord has been doing and is doing now in His recovery is bringing forth the one new man with Himself as the life, person, and constituent (Eph. 3:17-19; Col. 3:4, 10-11).

    B. The Lord wants to show Satan that He can produce and bring forth the one new man out of every tongue and people from among the nations; this is not an outward movement—it is Christ Himself within us as our life, person, and constituent (Rev. 5:9-10; Eph. 3:17; Col. 3:4, 10-11).

    C. The one new man will usher in the kingdom of God and will bring Christ, the King, back to the earth (Rev. 11:15).

Day 6

VI. Now is the time for God to accomplish His purpose—to perfect the one new man, who will come into full existence on earth (Eph. 4:24):

    A. The world situation has been raised up for the goal of bringing forth the one new man; everything that the Lord is doing in the present age is to usher in the practical existence of the one new man.

    B. When the one new man is full-grown and perfected, that will be the time for the Lord's coming, and the full-grown, perfected one new man will be the bride (vv. 12-13; Rev. 19:7).

C. "Today everything is ripe, ready, and prepared for the new man to come forth. We all have to see where we are. We are at the end time, and this is the most golden time. This is the right time for the Lord's recovery. Our view must be broadened" (*CWWL, 1977*, vol. 3, "The One New Man," p. 483).

D. "The Lord today is doing this work on the earth, and this is the goal of the Lord's recovery today" (*CWWL, 1977*, vol. 3, "One Body, One Spirit, and One New Man," p. 350).

Morning Nourishment

Prov. Where there is no vision, the people cast off re-
29:18 straint...
Acts   Therefore, King Agrippa, I was not disobedient to
26:19 the heavenly vision.
1 Cor. For even as the body is one and has many mem-
12:12 bers, yet all the members of the body, being many,
       are one body, so also is the Christ.

Before the Lord will be able to return, we must see the Body and
the new man. When we come to the end of the Bible, in Revelation 22,
the Spirit and the bride appear. At the end the new man is a bride.
The church's experience in Christ definitely must arrive at this
stage. First it is the Body, then it is the new man, and finally it is
the bride. It is not as some say in Christianity, that the believers
will be gathered into one place, and the Lord will change them in-
stantly into His bride. Instead, today we must receive grace to see
the Body, to see the new man, and finally to see the bride. (*CWWL,
1977,* vol. 3, "One Body, One Spirit, and One New Man," p. 314)

Today's Reading

Vision denotes an extraordinary scene. For example, someone
may have a house with exquisite decorations. Once you enter in
and take a look, you immediately sense something uncommon. To
you that is an uncommon scene; that is a vision. In the Bible *vision*
refers to the scenery we see from God. Through His Word God has
opened the veil, but we must see the scenes contained in the Word.
Whatever we see through God's revelation is a vision. (*CWWL,
1986,* vol. 3, "The Revelation and Vision of God," pp. 316-317)

I still remember the experience of the God of glory appearing to me for the first time. That was on the afternoon of the day
I was saved. When I walked out of the meeting hall into the
street, I felt that everything was different. I stopped by the road
and prayed to God, "God! I don't want anything else anymore. I
only want Yourself." This was the God of glory appearing to me.
I hope that in principle you would all have the same experience.
Do not be like the Christian missionaries. They serve the Lord

as a profession. I hope that everyone serving the Lord in His recovery would have this glorious vision breaking and shining upon him at least once. This is not a matter of any outward seeing. Rather, it is a definite and glorious inward seeing.

When I came back to Taiwan a few days ago, I received a call from one of the gospel teams. The brothers and sisters were very excited. They told me that within three weeks they had baptized eighty-two persons. The first Lord's Day they had twenty-three new ones attending their bread-breaking meeting. This is indeed encouraging. But we have to see that such excitement will ebb quickly if there is not a vision as the underlying support. It is like the weather that we have been experiencing these few days. At times a cold front comes, and the temperature goes down and up erratically. But if you have seen the vision, whether there is a cold front or a warm front, you will not be affected. We have to realize that we have the outreach in the villages because we have seen an inward vision. This glorious vision controls us and gives us the boldness to go on. (*CWWL, 1989,* vol. 1, "The Glorious Vision and the Way of the Cross," pp. 438, 440)

The Gospel of Mark is not merely a storybook. This Gospel conveys a heavenly vision, a vision that should direct our steps, control our living, and bring us into God's consummation. This vision is able to keep us in God's economy so that we may live the church life with the goal of reaching the millennium and the New Jerusalem.

Such a vision from God will always direct our steps and control our living. This was true even in the Old Testament, where we are told that without vision the people will cast off restraint (Prov. 29:18a). Under the heavenly vision we are directed toward God's destination, and our life is controlled according to God's economy. (*Life-study of Mark,* p. 452)

Further Reading: CWWL, 1977, vol. 3, "One Body, One Spirit, and One New Man," ch. 6; *CWWL, 1989,* vol. 1, "The Glorious Vision and the Way of the Cross," ch. 1

Enlightenment and inspiration: _Vision as the_
underlying support _____
_____
_____

Morning Nourishment

Gen. **And God said, Let Us make man in Our image,**
1:26 **according to Our likeness; and let them have do-**
     minion...
Eph. **That Christ may make His home in your hearts**
3:17 **through faith...**
4:23-24 **...Be renewed in the spirit of your mind and put on**
     the new man...

Ultimately, the Bible speaks of the church as the one new man. I cannot find any type that stands for the new man. In the Body we have the members; in the household we have the family members; in the assembly we have the assembly members. But what do we have in the man? The only thing is the person. In the new man there is nothing but the person. This level is so high that it cannot be higher, so strict that it cannot be stricter, and so intimate that it cannot be more intimate. All are one new man; this one new man has only one person, and this person is the Lord Jesus.

I am looking to the Lord from the depths of my being that at this time when saints from all the six continents are meeting together here, we would all seize the opportunity to see the highest meaning of the church revealed in the Bible. The highest definition of the church in the Bible is the new man. (*CWWL, 1977,* vol. 3, "One Body, One Spirit, and One New Man," pp. 332-333)

Today's Reading

It is easy for people to say that the church is the Body of Christ. However, the Bible says that the church is not only the Body but also the new man. The new man is different from the Body. Let us use the physical body as an example. A body is simply a vessel to be used as an organ. A man, however, is not merely an organ; a man has a person. A body needs life, but a man needs a person in addition to life. Life is different from a person. A plant has life, but it does not have a person. A man has not only life but also a person. In the past we saw that the church is the Body with Christ as its life. However, we did not see that the church is the new man with Christ not only as its life but also as its person.

The Bible says that the church is the new man. Ephesians 2:15 says that Christ abolished "in His flesh the law of the commandments in ordinances, that He might create the two in Himself into one new man, so making peace." Paul says that the Lord created the two—the Jewish and the Gentile believers—into one new man. Therefore, the new man is not an individual. The new man is corporate. (*CWWL, 1971,* vol. 1, "The Meaning of Human Life and a Proper Consecration," p. 199)

As the Body of Christ, the church needs Christ as its life. As the new man, the church needs Christ as its person. The body without life is not a body but a corpse. However, when the body makes a move, it is decided not by life but by the person. Hence, in the new man we need to take Christ as our person. The new man as a corporate person should live a life as Jesus lived on earth, that is, a life of truth, expressing God and causing God to be realized as reality by man. (*The Conclusion of the New Testament,* p. 2302)

Adam was a corporate man, a collective man, including all mankind. God did not create many men; He created mankind collectively in one person, Adam. God created such a corporate man in His image and according to His likeness so that mankind might express God corporately. (Gen. 1:26, footnote 4)

God created a corporate man not only to express Himself with His image but also to represent Him by exercising His dominion over all things. (Gen. 1:26, footnote 5)

God's creation of man in Genesis 1 is a picture of the new man in God's new creation. This means that the old creation is a figure, a type, of the new creation. In God's old creation the central character is man. It is the same in God's new creation. Therefore, in both the old creation and the new creation man is the center.

God created man in His own image (Gen. 1:26) and then gave man His dominion. (*The Conclusion of the New Testament,* p. 2302)

Further Reading: CWWL, 1971, vol. 1, "The Meaning of Human Life and a Proper Consecration," chs. 8-9

Enlightenment and inspiration: _____

_____

_____

_____

Morning Nourishment

Eph. Abolishing in His flesh the law of the command-
2:15-16 ments in ordinances, that He might create the two
in Himself into one new man, *so* making peace, and
might reconcile both in one Body to God through
the cross, having slain the enmity by it.

In God's creation of man there were two intentions. The positive intention is that man would bear God's image for His expression; the negative intention is that man would have God's dominion to represent Him to deal with His enemy.

In the old creation the dominion given to man was limited to the earth. This means that in the old creation the dealing with God's enemy was restricted to the earth. However, in God's new creation the dominion has been enlarged to the entire universe.

Eventually, the church as the new man is the man in God's intention. God wanted a man, and in the old creation He created a figure, a type, not the real man. The real man is the man Christ created on the cross through His all-inclusive death. This man is called the new man.

The term *the new man* reminds us of the old man. The old man did not fulfill God's dual purpose. However, the new man in God's new creation does fulfill the twofold purpose of expressing God and dealing with God's enemy. (*The Conclusion of the New Testament,* pp. 2302-2303)

Today's Reading

Anything in our daily life that does not have God in it is the old creation, but what has God in it is part of the new creation.

If we would be in the new creation, we must enter into an organic union with the Triune God. Apart from such a union we shall remain in the old creation. But now, by the organic union with the Triune God, we are in the new creation. As believers in Christ, we are the new creation through an organic union with the Triune God.

In Adam we were born into the old creation, but in Christ we were regenerated into the new creation. Here in the new creation we are not only God's assembly, God's house, and God's kingdom and not only Christ's Body and counterpart—we are also the new man. God's intention is to have a corporate, universal man. God wants such a man for the fulfillment of His eternal purpose. On the one hand, we were created in God's old creation and became the old man; on the other hand, we have been re-created in God's new creation and have become the new man. (*The Conclusion of the New Testament,* pp. 2304-2305) The Bible never says that there are many new men. The Bible tells us that there is only one new man (Eph. 2:15). This one new man is not an individual; he is a corporate man, and this corporate new man is the aggregate of all the God-men. When we put all the God-men together, we have one man. This one man is called "the new man" (Eph. 4:24; Col. 3:10), referring to the new mankind. Adam was the old mankind. All his descendants are one with him to be the old man. Today we, the believers in Christ, are all one with Christ to be the new man.

The new man was created by Christ with two kinds of materials. The first is the redeemed created man; the second is the divine element. On the cross Christ put these two materials together to produce a new man. If a grain of wheat is sown into the earth, on the one hand the grain of wheat will die. While it is dying, it is growing. The death of the grain of wheat brings forth a new plant. What was once only a grain of wheat eventually becomes a new plant that bears many grains of wheat (John 12:24). Through the death of the grain of wheat, the grain of wheat is terminated. At the same time, something is germinated that grows up to be a new plant. This is an illustration of what was accomplished in Christ's death. While He was on the cross, Christ was terminating, and He was also begetting. (*The God-men,* pp. 16-18)

Further Reading: The Conclusion of the New Testament, msg. 216; *CWWL, 1970,* vol. 3, "Taking Christ as Our Person for the Church Life," ch. 4

Enlightenment and inspiration: _____

_____

_____

_____

Morning Nourishment

Col. **And have put on the new man, which is being**
3:10-11 **renewed unto full knowledge according to the**
image of Him who created him, where there can-
not be Greek and Jew, circumcision and uncir-
cumcision, barbarian, Scythian, slave, free man,
but Christ is all and in all.

Since death ushers us into resurrection, in His resurrection Christ put us into Himself. Then with His divine essence He created us in Himself into the one new man.

Ephesians 2:15 does not say, "That He might create the two into one new man." Do not ignore the phrase *in Himself.* Apart from being in Him, we could not have been created into the new man, because in ourselves we do not have the divine essence, which is the element of the new man. Only in the divine essence and with the divine essence were we created into the new man. It is possible to have this essence only in Christ. In fact, Christ Himself is this essence, this element. Hence, in Himself Christ created the two into one new man. We all need to be profoundly impressed with the fact that we, the believers, have been created into one new man in Christ. (*Life-study of Ephesians,* pp. 211-212)

Today's Reading

Putting on the new man does not take place once for all. On the contrary, it is a lifelong matter, a gradual process that goes on throughout our Christian life....The new man has been created in Christ and with Christ. In Ephesians 2:15, the Greek word rendered "in" has an instrumental significance; it also means "with." Thus, in Himself actually means with Himself. The new man has already been created with Christ as the divine essence. When we were regenerated, this new man was put into our spirit. Now day by day we need to put on this new man by permitting the spirit to control our being and renew our mind. Every time part of our being is renewed, we put on a little more of the new man. Hence, the more we are renewed through the spirit controlling our mind, the more of the new man we put on. Eventually, this process of putting on the new man will be completed.

In the one new man there are none of the national and cultural distinctions between the peoples. Here there is neither Jew nor Gentile, slave nor free man, cultured nor uncultured (Col. 3:10-11). Likewise, there is no American, nor British, nor Japanese, nor Chinese, nor German, nor French. In this new man Christ is all because He is the very essence with which the new man is created. Hence, the new man is just Christ. (*Life-study of Ephesians*, p. 214)

In Colossians Paul presents the Christ who is the fullness of the invisible God. After mentioning aspect after aspect of such a Christ, he speaks of the new man. Between Christ as the fullness of God in chapter 1 and the new man in chapter 3 we have the experience of Christ and the enjoyment of Him. The issue of our experience and enjoyment of the all-inclusive Christ is the church as the new man. Hence, the new man comes out of our enjoyment of Christ as the fullness of God. As we enjoy Christ daily, He is wrought into us, constituted into our very being. In this way, Christ becomes our constituent. Day by day, Christ is being constituted into us. Eventually, we all shall be thoroughly constituted of Him. As a result of being constituted of Christ, we become the new man. In this new man there is no place for any natural person; there is room only for Christ. Christ is all and in all in the new man....In the new man Christ is all the members and is in all the members.

The only way Christ can be all and in all in the new man is for Him to constitute Himself into us. The process of being constituted of Christ takes place through our enjoyment of Christ.... As we call on the Lord, praise Him, and offer Him our thanks and adoration, we are filled with Him. Through such an enjoyment of Christ and experience of Him, we are gradually constituted of Christ. It is as we enjoy Him that He constitutes us of Himself. (*Life-study of Colossians*, pp. 508-509)

Further Reading: Life-study of Ephesians, msg. 24; *Life-study of Colossians,* msg. 28

Enlightenment and inspiration: _____

_____
_____
_____

Morning Nourishment

Eph. **That you put off, as regards your former manner of**
4:22-23 **life, the old man, which is being corrupted accord-**
ing to the lusts of the deceit, and *that* you be
renewed in the spirit of your mind.

The new man has not yet come into fullness. Years ago,
I met some dear missionaries who happily told me that the
gospel had been brought to every continent and every corner of
the earth. However, God cannot be so happy because He still
has not reached His goal. God's goal is not that the gospel be
preached in every corner of the earth. His goal is to have the
new man. The new man is a replacement of the old man. For
the replacement of the old man, the new man must be constituted with every people, every tribe, and every nation. In this
sense, it was not possible to have the new man to the extent
that it is possible today. (*CWWL, 1977*, vol. 3, "The One New
Man," p. 480)

Today's Reading

At this end time the Lord is going to bring forth the new
man. The Lord today is going to raise up His believers throughout all the world, in so many countries, to seek after Him. When
we seek after Him, we will see that what He wants is such a
new man.

The new man is not a movement, such as the ecumenical
movement, and is not an organization but a man. As a man, the
new man must have life, and he must have a person. The life of
this new man must be Christ, and the person of this new man
must also be Christ. In this new man there is no place for anyone else. The Jew, the Greek, the circumcised, the uncircum-
cised, the barbarian, the Scythian, the slave, and the free man
all have no place, but Christ is all and in all (Col. 3:11). For one
to say that Christ is his life and Christ is his person is not good
enough. We must say in the plural that Christ is our life and
Christ is our person. The Lord's recovery is here to bring forth
the new man. In the Lord's recovery the Lord does not care for a

movement or an organization. What He has been doing, and what He is now doing, is bringing forth the new man with Himself as the life and person. (*CWWL, 1977,* vol. 3, "The One New Man," p. 497)

Today we all must see that this is not merely a conference of all the continents in which we decide what we all will speak about from now on. Absolutely not. Instead, it is a matter of all of us seeing that the Lord is our life and our person. The Lord today wants to show Satan that He can produce the one new man out of every tongue and people from among the nations. It is not an outward teaching or an outward movement, but it is He Himself within us as life and as our person. We all receive Him and grow up into Him in all things, and then the whole Body is joined and knit together out from Him.

When we grow up into Christ in all things, the entire Body will be joined and knit together out from Him. When we grow up into Him and come out from Him, then we will be completely in Him and not in ourselves....When we grow up into Him and come out from Him, we are easily joined and knit together. You and I and all of us must grow up into Him, pass through Him, and come out from Him; then there will be this new man. (*CWWL, 1977,* vol. 3, "One Body, One Spirit, and One New Man," pp. 348-349)

All the fullness of God is embodied in Christ, and this Christ is wrought into our being to be our righteousness, our holiness, our love, and our light. This is the new man with the new man's expression. Such a new man with such an expression will usher in the kingdom of God and will bring Christ, the King, back to this earth. The goal of the Lord's recovery is to become such a new man, which is the very expression of God. (*CWWL, 1977,* vol. 3, "The One New Man," p. 501)

Further Reading: CWWL, 1977, vol. 3, "The One New Man," ch. 2; *CWWL, 1977,* vol. 3, "One Body, One Spirit, and One New Man," ch. 5

Enlightenment and inspiration: _____

_____

_____

_____

Morning Nourishment

Eph. Until we all arrive at the oneness of the faith and
4:13 of the full knowledge of the Son of God, at a full-
grown man, at the measure of the stature of the
fullness of Christ.

24 And put on the new man, which was created according to God in righteousness and holiness of
the reality.

Today the situation on the earth has been very much im-
proved and made ready and ripe to have the new man. At the
time of the apostle Paul it was not like this. Paul did not have a
brother among the American Indians, but in the new man today
we do have brothers and sisters from among the Indians. Eventually, I believe that among the Indian reservations there will be
some churches in the Lord's recovery. The world situation has
been raised up for the one goal of the new man. Now we have different peoples all mingled together in the one new man. (*CWWL,
1977,* vol. 3, "The One New Man," p. 482)

Today's Reading

God's purpose is to have a man to express Him and to exercise
His dominion. The old man failed God, but God has raised up a new
man to replace the old man. Still even today we could not see a perfect new man on the earth to replace the fallen old man. However,
our God can never be defeated. Now is the very time for Him to accomplish His purpose to perfect the new man. This new man will
come into full existence on the earth. God needs such a man to express Himself and to exercise His dominion. When this new man is
perfected, that will be the time of the Lord's coming, and the perfected new man will be the bride. We need such a vision.

Such a vision will not only keep us in oneness but also will
deliver us and rescue us from all things other than Christ. We
need such a vision. Throughout the years some have said in a
narrow way that each local church must have its own jurisdic-
tion and its own autonomy, but we need to see that all the local
churches in the different countries are one new man.

According to history and according to the Bible, culture always goes along with God's intention. Even though the fallen human culture is not of God, God is sovereign over all these things. God has brought human culture from the sea to the ocean and above the ocean to the skies for the purpose of perfecting the new man. Everything on this earth is for the perfection of the new man. Today with the world politics, scientific inventions, modern transportation and communication, and our understanding of languages, the world has been condensed into a small sphere. There is nearly no hindrance for the new man to be perfected. Today everything is ripe, ready, and prepared for the new man to come forth. We all have to see where we are. We are at the end time, and this is the most golden time. This is the right time for the Lord's recovery. Our view must be broadened. There is only one new man, and nothing and no one has any place in this new man, but Christ is all and in all. (*CWWL, 1977,* vol. 3, "The One New Man," pp. 482-483)

The life-giving Spirit enters our spirit to process us, and this processing is transformation because the element of the Spirit increases. It is this mingled spirit—the spirit that is two spirits becoming one spirit—that seeps out of our spirit and soaks through our mind, emotion, and will, even our entire being. In this way we are renewed in this spirit of our mind. The renewing makes us all into the new man. In this renewing we put off the old social life and put on the church life. This is putting off the old man and putting on the new man.

The Lord today is doing this work on the earth, and this is the goal of the Lord's recovery today. All those who love Him, pursue Him, and follow Him on the entire earth today must be renewed in the spirit of their mind to become the one new man, taking Him as their person and living by Him. This is what the Lord wants today. (*CWWL, 1977,* vol. 3, "One Body, One Spirit, and One New Man," p. 350)

Further Reading: One Body, One Spirit, and One New Man, ch. 7;
   CWWL, 1972, vol. 1, "The Four Men in the Bible," ch. 3

Enlightenment and inspiration: _____

_____

_____

_____

Hymns, #1230

1   One new man is the Father's plan;
    He redeemed us from the sons of men.
    Every kindred, tribe and tongue,
    In Himself He called us to be one.
    God's expression on the earth
    Now reveals His glorious worth.
    One new man is the Father's plan;
    He redeemed us from the sons of men.

2   On the cross ordinances slain,
    That He might form just one of twain.
    Reconciling us to God,
    Thus on the serpent's head He trod.
    He breaks down the middle wall
    As upon His name we call;
    On the cross ordinances slain,
    That He might form just one of twain.

3   For this cause Your person, Lord,
    We take and stand in one accord;
    All the members self forsake,
    And of the Body-Christ partake.
    We in Christ as one new man
    Now come forth to take this land.
    For this cause Your person, Lord,
    We take and stand in one accord.

Composition for prophecy with main point and sub-points: _____

66. *Saints from*
> 60 *nations came together for the*
ICPC
→ *a picture of one new man*

Being Renewed in the Spirit of the Mind for the Practical Existence of the One New Man

Scripture Reading: Eph. 2:15-16; 4:22-24; Col. 3:10-11; Rom. 12:2

Day 1

I. Everything that the Lord is doing in this present age is to usher in the practical existence of the one new man; this is the Lord's move on earth today (Eph. 2:15; 4:24; Col. 3:10-11).

II. In our experience as believers in Christ, we should cooperate with the Triune God to put off the old man, which was terminated on the cross, and put on the new man, which was created through Christ's death and resurrection (Eph. 2:15; 4:22, 24):

A. Regarding our former manner of life, we must put off the old man (v. 22):

1. In baptism we put off the old man; our old man was crucified with Christ and was buried in baptism (Rom. 6:4a, 6).

2. The former manner of life was a walk in the vanity of the mind (Eph. 4:22, 17):

   a. The former manner of life includes everything related to us, especially the community life of the old man (v. 22).

   b. To put off regarding the "former manner of life, the old man" is to put off our way of living (v. 22).

3. The old man "is being corrupted according to the lusts of the deceit" (v. 22):

   a. The article before *deceit* is emphatic, and *the deceit* is personified.

   b. *The deceit* refers to the deceiver, Satan, from whom come the lusts of the corrupted old man.

B. We need to "put on the new man, which was created according to God in righteousness and holiness of the reality" (v. 24):

1. In baptism we put on the new man (Rom. 6:4b).
2. The new man is of Christ; it is His Body created in Him on the cross (Eph. 2:15-16).

Day 2

3. To put on the new man is to put on the community life of the one new man (4:24):
   a. To put on the church life as the one new man is to put on a corporate entity produced by the mingling of the divine Spirit with the regenerated human spirit (1 Cor. 15:45b; 6:17).
   b. Since we are part of the one new man, our living should be the living of the one new man as the corporate God-man (Eph. 4:17-32).
4. *The reality* in Ephesians 4:24 is the personification of God; the reality is God; it was in the righteousness and holiness of the reality that the one new man was created.

Day 3

III. The key to putting off the old man and putting on the new man is in being renewed in the spirit of our mind (v. 23):
   A. Christ as the life-giving Spirit is now in our spirit, and these two spirits mingle together to form the spirit of the mind (2 Tim. 4:22; 1 Cor. 6:17).
   B. When the life-giving Spirit, who dwells in and is mingled with our regenerated spirit, spreads into our mind, this mingled spirit becomes the spirit of the mind; it is by this mingled spirit that our mind is renewed (Eph. 4:23).
   C. To be renewed in the spirit of our mind is inward and intrinsic; the renewing in the spirit of our mind revolutionizes our logic, philosophy, thought, concept, and psychology (Rom. 12:2).

Day 4

   D. The only possibility of God's purpose being fulfilled in this age is that we all would be willing to be renewed in the spirit of our mind (Eph. 3:11; 4:23).

IV. **The renewal of the mind is for the practical existence of the one new man (vv. 22-24; Col. 3:10-11):**

A. The only way that the one new man can be realized practically is by our mind being renewed (Rom. 12:2; Eph. 4:23-24; Col. 3:10-11).

B. We need to be renewed in the spirit of our mind actually and daily in our living; otherwise, there is no way for the Lord to have the one new man.

C. Our mind needs to be renewed not only for our spiritual conduct or for our personal, ethical behavior but for the existence of the one new man (Eph. 4:24).

Day 5

D. The focal point of our being renewed in the spirit of our mind is the one new man (vv. 23-24).

E. Throughout our life, our national and racial mentality has been built up, and for the existence of the one new man, this mentality must be renewed (v. 23):

1. Our natural and national mentality was educated and built up according to our racial and cultural background; this is the greatest hindrance to the practical existence of the one new man (Col. 3:10-11).

2. In order for the one new man to come into full existence, we must experience a thorough renewal of our mind, which has been built up according to our nationality and culture (Rom. 12:2; Eph. 4:23-24; Col. 3:10-11).

Day 6

F. In our prayer we need to have a desire to enter into the practicality of the one new man, and thus, we need to ask the Lord to renew our mind and transform our inner being (Rom. 12:2).

G. Daily we need to put off the old man and put on the new man; for this we need to drink of the one Spirit so that we may be renewed in the spirit of our mind in every area of our daily life (1 Cor. 12:13):

1. When we drink of the Spirit, He saturates

every part of our being; the first part of our
soul that He saturates is our mind (v. 13;
Rom. 12:2).

2. If we drink of the Spirit, we will be renewed
in the spirit of our mind, and this renewing
will make us all into one new man (Eph.
4:23-24).

3. When our mind has been renewed, the one
new man will come into existence in a practical way, and Christ will truly be all and in
all (Col. 3:10-11).

H. "All those who love Him, pursue Him, and follow
Him on the entire earth today must be renewed
in the spirit of their mind to become the one new
man, taking Him as their person and living by
Him. This is what the Lord wants today" (*CWWL,
1977*, vol. 3, "One Body, One Spirit, and One New
Man," p. 350).

Morning Nourishment

Rom. Knowing this, that our old man has been crucified
6:6 with *Him* in order that the body of sin might be
     annulled, that we should no longer serve sin as
     slaves.

Eph. Abolishing in His flesh the law of the command-
2:15 ments in ordinances, that He might create the two
     in Himself into one new man, *so* making peace.

The Lord prophesied in Matthew 16:18 that He would build His church. Whatever the Lord has prophesied must be fulfilled. Without the practical existence of the new man, the building up of the church may be vain talk. The building of the church depends upon the existence of the new man. If the new man comes into existence, no doubt, the builded church is here. Regardless of the present situation of division, the Lord is going to get the new man. Everything that the Lord is doing in this present age is to usher in the practical existence of the one new man. To drop our natural, religious concepts, our mind needs to be saturated, permeated, possessed, and taken over by our mingled spirit. Then our concepts will be fully revolutionized, and we will no longer have any ordinances. The new man will then come into existence. This is the Lord's move on the earth today. (*CWWL, 1977*, vol. 3, "The One New Man," p. 520)

Today's Reading

The goal of God's New Testament economy is to gain the new man. The old man failed God, so in His New Testament economy God is going to get a new man. For this purpose Christ died on the cross not only to take away our sins, to crucify our old man, to destroy Satan, and to judge the world, but also to abolish the ordinances, the different ways of living among different peoples, so that He could create in Himself a new man. All the different ways of living and worship were abolished on the cross. (*CWWL, 1977*, vol. 3, "The One New Man," p. 521)

In Ephesians 4:22 Paul says, "You put off, as regards your former manner of life, the old man, which is being corrupted according to the lusts of the deceit." In verse 24 Paul goes on to say, "Put on the new man, which was created according to God in righteousness and holiness of the reality." It is based upon our having put off the old man and having put on the new man that we can enjoy Christ as the reality and grace for the living of the new man. In our experience, we should cooperate with the Triune God to put off the old man, which He terminated on the cross; we should also cooperate with the Triune God to put on the new man, which He created through Christ's death and resurrection.

Verse 22 says that we have put off, as regards the former manner of life, the old man. The former manner of life was a walk in the vanity of the mind. Such a manner of life has been terminated and put away. Verse 22 also says that the old man "is being corrupted according to the lusts of the deceit." The old man is of Adam, who was created by God but fallen through sin. The article before the word *deceit* is emphatic and indicates that *the deceit* is personified. Hence, *deceit* here refers to the deceiver, the devil, from whom are the lusts of the corrupted old man. The old man is corrupted according to the lusts of the devil, the deceiving one. Outwardly, the manner of life of the old man is a walk in the vanity of the mind. Inwardly, the old man is corrupted according to the lusts of the devil, the lusts of the deceit. This old man was crucified with Christ (Rom. 6:6) and was buried in baptism (v. 4). We should praise the Lord that we have put off the old man in baptism.

It was [also] in baptism that we put on the new man (v. 4b). The new man is the practical church life, which is Christ as the life-giving Spirit mingled with our spirit in a corporate way. To put on the church life as the new man is to put on this entity produced by the mingling of the divine Spirit with the human spirit. (*The Conclusion of the New Testament*, pp. 3433-3434)

Further Reading: The Conclusion of the New Testament, msg. 341; *Truth Lessons—Level Three*, vol. 4, lsn. 63

Enlightenment and inspiration: _____

_____

_____

_____

Morning Nourishment

Eph. That you put off, as regards your former manner of
4:22 life, the old man, which is being corrupted according to the lusts of the deceit.

24 And put on the new man, which was created according to God in righteousness and holiness of
the reality.

Because the book of Ephesians is a book on the church, we
should view everything in it from the perspective of the church. If
we fail to do this, we shall wrongly apply many things in this book.
As we read 4:17-32, we should apply these verses corporately, not
individualistically. These verses are not written in relation to the
lives of individuals but in relation to the corporate life of the one
new man. The new man must become our daily living. In verse 24
Paul speaks of putting on the new man. To put on the new man
means to have the church life, which is the new life of the new
mankind created by Christ in Himself. The church is a new
humanity. Corporately we need to put on another humanity. It is
crucial for us to have this view as we consider the second half of
Ephesians 4. (*Life-study of Ephesians,* p. 777)

Today's Reading

To put off the old man is not merely to put off the old nature;
it is to put off the old way of life, the former way of living. Our
old way of living was not entirely an individualistic way of life,
for it involved our social life, our community life. No human
being can be altogether individualistic. Human nature is in-
herently social. To be a human being is to live in society and to
have some kind of community life.

In the church we have the best community life. If there were
no church meetings, we would feel aimless, and our existence
would be meaningless. We enjoy coming together in the meetings. The fact that the saints often linger after the meetings are
dismissed indicates that in the church we have a genuine community life. If we would be the one new man, we must put off
the community life of the old man and put on the community

life of the new man. (*Life-study of Ephesians,* p. 777)

The believers experience the dispensing of the processed Triune God corporately by putting on the new man (Eph. 4:22-24). The new man is of Christ. It is His Body, created in Him on the cross (2:15-16). It is not individual but corporate (Col. 3:10-11).

The phrase "in Himself" in Ephesians 2:15 is very significant. It indicates that Christ was not only the Creator of the one new man, the church, but also the sphere in which and the essence with which the one new man was created. Christ is the very element of the new man. Nothing of our old man was good for the creation of the new man, for our former essence was sinful. But in Christ there is a wonderful essence, in which the one new man has been created. This new man, which is the church, is corporate and universal. There are many believers, but there is only one new man in the universe. All the believers are components of this one corporate and universal new man.

Outwardly everything related to the new man is righteous, and inwardly everything related to the new man is holy.

In 4:24 righteousness signifies God's deeds, and holiness signifies His being. Whatever God does is righteous, and whatever God is, is holy. The new man is created according to God in both of these respects.

The righteousness and holiness of the new man are of "the reality." The article before "reality" in verse 24 is emphatic. As the deceit in verse 22, related to the old man, is the personification of Satan, so reality here, related to the new man, is the personification of God. This reality was exhibited in the life of Jesus, as mentioned in verse 21. In the life of Jesus righteousness and holiness of reality were always being manifested. It was in the righteousness and holiness of this reality, which is God realized and expressed, that the new man was created. (*The Conclusion of the New Testament,* pp. 1809-1810, 1814)

Further Reading: The Conclusion of the New Testament, msg. 166; *Life-study of Ephesians,* msgs. 24-25, 47

Enlightenment and inspiration: _____

_____

_____

_____

Morning Nourishment

Rom. And do not be fashioned according to this age, but
12:2 be transformed by the renewing of the mind that
you may prove what the will of God is, that which
is good and well pleasing and perfect.

Eph. And *that* you be renewed in the spirit of your mind.
4:23

To have the practice of the new man we must know who
Christ is and where Christ is. Christ today is the life-giving
Spirit (1 Cor. 15:45b; 2 Cor. 3:17), and He is in our spirit (Rom.
8:16; 2 Tim. 4:22). The life-giving Spirit, Christ, is now in our
spirit, and these two spirits mingle together to form the spirit of
the mind (Eph. 4:23). Ephesians 4:23 says that we are being
renewed in the spirit of our mind. Our mind is being renewed
through our realization that Christ as the life-giving Spirit is
mingled with our human spirit.

It is uncommon today to hear a message concerning the mingled spirit or on being renewed in the spirit of the mind. Some
who have never heard of the mingled spirit may teach that it is
sufficient for us to read the Bible, win souls, and glorify God by
our good behavior. However, Ephesians 4:23 is vital and crucial
to us. The key to putting off the old man (v. 22) and putting on the
new man (v. 24) is in being renewed in the spirit of our mind.
(*CWWL, 1977,* vol. 3, "The One New Man," p. 491)

Today's Reading

As believers, we can experience and enjoy Christ as the reality and grace for the living of the new man through the renewing
in the spirit of our mind [Eph. 4:23]....Our being renewed is for
our transformation into the image of Christ (Rom. 12:2; 2 Cor.
3:18). The spirit here is the regenerated spirit of the believers,
which is mingled with the indwelling Spirit of God. Such a mingled spirit spreads into our mind, thus becoming the spirit of our
mind. It is in such a spirit that we are renewed for our transformation. This, of course, implies a process of metabolic transformation. As this process takes place, the mingled spirit enters our
mind, takes over our mind, and becomes the spirit of our mind.

When our human spirit is regenerated by and thus mingled with the Spirit of God, it becomes the mingled spirit. When our regenerated spirit is gradually enlightened, motivated, inspired, and occupied by the Spirit of God, the mingled spirit spreads into our mind and becomes the spirit of our mind. At the time of regeneration the mingled spirit is only in the realm of our spirit; through renewing, this mingled spirit progressively moves into the territory of our mind to become the spirit of our mind. It is by the spirit spreading into our mind that we are renewed in order that the new man would live on earth.

As those who love Christ, we should not have vanity in our mind; instead, we should have the spirit in our mind. Our mind should no longer be full of vanity; rather, it should be saturated with the mingled spirit. (*The Conclusion of the New Testament,* pp. 3432-3433)

To be renewed in the spirit of our mind is inward and intrinsic. If we learn to be renewed in this way, we will have a deeper perception with which to understand persons and matters. To understand a person requires that we have a deeper sight, a perception that goes farther and deeper. Often our knowing of people is shallow. We lack the perception that penetrates the barriers and coverings because we do not practice being daily renewed in the spirit of our mind. The renewing in the spirit of our mind always revolutionizes our logic, philosophy, thought, concept, and psychology. As a result, our perception in all things is different, and we have a deeper understanding of the people we meet. Even by the way they ask questions, we can know people's condition. A natural man is a very shallow man, but if we are spiritual, we will be deep. If we are deep, we will know others, even though they will not be able to know us (1 Cor. 2:15). (*CWWL, 1990,* vol. 2, "Messages to the Trainees in Fall 1990," p. 453)

Further Reading: The Believer's Experience of Transformation, ch. 4; *CWWL, 1977,* vol. 3, "The One New Man," ch. 5

Enlightenment and inspiration: _____

_____

_____

_____

spirit spread into our mind

Morning Nourishment

Eph. And *that* you be renewed in the spirit of your mind
4:23-24 and put on the new man, which was created according to God in righteousness and holiness of
the reality.

Not only is there no natural person in the new man, but
there is no possibility, no room, for any natural person. In the
new man there is room only for Christ. He is all the members of
the new man and in all the members. He is everything in the
new man. Actually, He is the new man, His Body (1 Cor. 12:12).
In the new man He is the centrality and universality.

The only possibility of the Lord's eternal purpose being fulfilled in this age is if we would all be willing to be renewed in
the spirit of our mind. This means that we have to open up ourselves and drink of the Spirit in order that the Spirit may get
into our being, saturating our natural mentality so that we can
have a metabolic change in our way of life. Then there is much
possibility for the new man to come into full existence. (*CWWL,
1977*, vol. 3, "The One New Man," pp. 510-511)

Today's Reading

The only way the one new man can be realized practically is
by our mind being renewed. The one new man cannot be realized by our being corrected or taught but by the Spirit of God
permeating our mentality.

I believe that the Lord's grace will work in us and upon us to
such an extent that we are being renewed in the spirit of our
mind not only when we are praying but also while we are living
our daily life. When we pray ourselves into the spirit, we are
being renewed. Peter was renewed in the trance that he had,
but in practice Peter had a problem. Today it is the same with
us. When we pray, we pray ourselves into the spirit, but we have
to keep ourselves all the time in our spirit in our daily life. Do
not let yourself come out of the spirit.

Through this fellowship we can see how much renewal we
need in all the matters of our daily life. The husbands need to

be renewed in their relationships with their wives. Do not be what you have habitually been. You have to be renewed in the spirit of your mind actually and daily in your living. Otherwise, there is no way for the Lord to have the Body, and no way for Him to have the new man. This is not a matter of adjusting our behavior but a matter of being transformed by being renewed in the spirit of our mind to make us another person. Daily we need to put off the old man and put on the new man. For this we need to drink of the one Spirit so that we may be renewed in the spirit of our mind in every area of our practical, daily life.

We need to be renewed in our mind not just for our personal, ethical behavior but for the one new man. Many Christians today still hold on to their natural, religious, and individual concepts because they will not let the Spirit spread into their mind....We all need to open ourselves up to the Lord and pray, "Lord, I am here. I want my mind to be fully opened to You. Come in and fill me up. Permeate, saturate, and possess my entire inward being." I believe that if we would pray to the Lord in such a way, the Spirit would have a way to permeate our mind. When the Spirit permeates our mind, the ordinances are over. When the Spirit has possessed and saturated our mind, we will not care for black, white, Chinese, Japanese, American, British, German, French, Italian, or Spanish. We will not care whether the meeting is noisy or quiet. We will only care for the one new man.

The church is the new man. Even though in this modern era so many races and peoples have been brought together, people still like to keep themselves divided. To keep ourselves divided from other Christians because of religious ordinances is to be conformed to this age because this age is one of division....We need to interpret Romans 12:2 in the way of not being conformed to this age of division. We Christians are one. (*CWWL, 1977,* vol. 3, "The One New Man," pp. 520, 529-530, 519-520)

Further Reading: CWWL, 1977, vol. 3, "One Body, One Spirit, and One New Man," chs. 8-9

Enlightenment and inspiration: _____

_____

_____

_____

Morning Nourishment

Col. **And have put on the new man, which is being**
3:10-11 **renewed unto full knowledge according to the**
        image of Him who created him, where there can-
        not be Greek and Jew, circumcision and uncircum-
        cision, barbarian, Scythian, slave, free man, but
        Christ is all and in all.

When I was a young believer, I thought that the renewing in the spirit of our mind was just for our Christian behavior. We can get our mind renewed by allowing it to be filled, possessed, and taken over by the Spirit of God. We have to pray, to fellowship with the Lord, to call on His name, and even to make a thorough confession of our sins. Then we will be transformed, and our behavior will be changed. Although this is true, the focal point of being renewed in the spirit of our mind is for the one new man. (*CWWL, 1977,* vol. 3, "The One New Man," p. 516)

Today's Reading

In the new man Greek and Jew, circumcision and uncircumcision, barbarian, Scythian, slave, and free man have no place. The renewal is not merely for our behavior. The renewal is…to get rid of our racial ordinances and to get rid of the natural persons.…We all need to be renewed for the existence of the one new man.

When the Spirit spreads into our mind, it becomes the spirit of our mind. It is in such a Spirit that we are renewed for our transformation. The Spirit renews, reconstructs, rearranges, our mind. Man is absolutely under the control and direction of his mind. What his mind thinks, he does,…he follows,…[and] he carries out. The director of our being is our mind. Even after you have been regenerated and are loving the Lord, you are still under the direction of your mind.

We need to drink of the one Spirit so that the Spirit can saturate our mind. The renewal of the mind is for the real practice of the new man. The British, the Chinese, and the Americans all have different ordinances related to their culture. This is why we need to have our national mentality renewed. Our national and even natural mentality was educated and built up according to our racial and cultural background. This is the top hindrance to the existence of the new man. Brother Hudson Taylor went to China with a burden to bring the gospel to the Chinese. He was so burdened that he even dressed the way the Chinese did. This was very commendable, but we must go further to see that it is necessary to be renewed in our mentality. Merely to change in an outward way could be a kind of performance and not the renewal in our mind.

We believe that this is the age for the new man to be perfected and to come into existence in a full way. The Lord has arranged the outward environment and situation for the new man to come into being, but the outward situation has to match the inward reality. There is the need of the inward reality in the members of the Body of Christ. Due to the scientific inventions and the political situations on this earth, the many nationalities and cultures have been brought together. Now there is the need of the inward reality, which is the renewal of our mind. Our national, racial mentality, which has been built up through our entire life, must be renewed.

[When I first] came to the United States, the Lord showed me that I had to give up my Chinese mentality. I wanted a mind that cared only for the Lord's recovery and not for my Chinese way of living. We need the Lord's mercy and grace for Him to renew our mind. The Lord is going to perform something to bring this one new man into full existence. The Lord is going to do such a marvelous thing with all the different cultures and races. The tendency of this age is pointed toward the Lord's work for the one new man. But in order for this to happen, we must have a thorough, proper, and adequate renewal of our mind, which has been built up by our nationality. This is why we have to drink of the Spirit. Then our entire being, especially our mind, will be saturated by the Spirit. (*CWWL, 1977,* vol. 3, "The One New Man," pp. 516-517, 507-509)

Further Reading: CWWL, 1971, vol. 1, "The Meaning of Human Life and a Proper Consecration," chs. 8-9; *God's Intention concerning Christ and the Church,* ch. 9

Enlightenment and inspiration: _____

_____

_____

_____

Morning Nourishment

1 Cor. For also in one Spirit we were all baptized into one
12:13 Body, whether Jews or Greeks, whether slaves or
free, and were all given to drink one Spirit.
Rev. And the Spirit and the bride say, Come! And let him
22:17 who hears say, Come! And let him who is thirsty
come; let him who wills take the water of life freely.

Humanly speaking, there is no possibility of getting rid of the differences between the races. In addition to our national character, each one of us has a particular character and disposition since we were raised in different environments and come from different backgrounds. Without the Lord's grace and without the Spirit, no one could be one with anyone else. We may have the doctrine. We may have listened to a message concerning the one new man. We may have received and accepted the vision of the one new man. But what about our practical, daily living? Are we day by day really under the renewing in the spirit of our mind? The matter of renewing is very practical. If you are really renewed, this will be seen in your practical, daily life. When the Lord saved us, we began to love Him. Now we realize that we have to practice the proper church life in putting on the one new man. This is why we need to ask the Lord to renew our mind and transform our inward being. (*CWWL, 1977,* vol. 3, "The One New Man," p. 528)

Today's Reading

In our prayer we must have a desire to get into the practicality of the new man. We need to ask the Lord to show us what the real practical problem is in our daily living for our fellowship with all the saints, for our church life. I believe that if we ask the Lord to shine on us in this way, He will point out many things.

As long as we have the baptism in the Spirit and the constant drinking, we will also have a thorough renewal. Whatever we drink saturates, refreshes, and renews our physical body. In like manner, when we drink the Spirit, He saturates every part of our inner being. Just to have the baptism in the Spirit is not adequate. We need the inward saturation, so we need to drink of the

Spirit. If we drink of the Spirit, we will be renewed in the spirit of our mind (Eph. 4:23). We do not just need an outward baptism but an inward, constant, and instant drinking of the Spirit into our very inward being. When we drink of the one Spirit, this Spirit saturates our inward being. The leading and central part of our inward being is the mind. Thus, when the Spirit has been drunk into us, it first saturates our mind.

Some of the saints are frustrated in their spiritual drinking. Their drinking of the Spirit fluctuates. At times they will drink a lot, and at other times they will not drink for a week. If our drinking of the Spirit is inconsistent and irregular, we cannot have a healthy spiritual situation. Without drinking, it is hard to be healthy. The more we drink, the more we bring in the existence of the one new man.

When the element of God gets into our mentality, we will think as He thinks, we will see things the way He does, and we will consider the situation as He does. It is then that the one new man will come into existence. There will be no races, no social ranks, and no religious differences. Christ will truly be all and in all. I believe that this is the up-to-date vision of the Lord's move on this earth. The Lord is moving on to get the one new man. (*CWWL, 1977,* vol. 3, "The One New Man," pp. 528, 507, 515, 520)

The renewing makes us all into the new man. In this renewing we put off the old social life and put on the church life. This is putting off the old man and putting on the new man.

The Lord today is doing this work on the earth, and this is the goal of the Lord's recovery today. All those who love Him, pursue Him, and follow Him on the entire earth today must be renewed in the spirit of their mind to become the one new man, taking Him as their person and living by Him. This is what the Lord wants today. (*CWWL, 1977,* vol. 3, "One Body, One Spirit, and One New Man," p. 350)

Further Reading: CWWL, 1977, vol. 3, "The One New Man," chs. 6-7

Enlightenment and inspiration: _____

_____
_____
_____

Hymns, #823

2   To the throne Christ has ascended,
       Far above all rule and power;
    God has made Him Head o'er all things
       To the church, His Body here.
    All in all He ever filleth,
       And His fullness is expressed
    Through the church, which is His Body
       And His image manifests.

3   We, once dead in our offenses,
       Walking in the worldly course,
    Lusts of flesh and mind fulfilling,
       Satan and his hosts their source,
    God with Christ has resurrected,
       Seated in the heavenlies;
    We, His masterpiece, created
       In Christ Jesus, Him to please.

4   Jews and Gentiles are one Body—
       God His myst'ry has made known—
    On apostles, prophets founded,
       Jesus Christ the cornerstone;
    We in Him are built together
       For God's dwelling manifest,
    Fitly framed by God the Spirit
       For His pleasure and His rest.

6   One in Body, hope, and Spirit,
       One in faith, one Lord, the Son,
    One baptizing, with one Father,
       That the church may thus be one;
    Christ to know in all His fullness,
       Unto manhood be matured,
    Ne'er by winds of doctrine carried,
       Nor by cunning men allured.

7   Many gifts the Lord has given,
       That His Body He may build,
    That the saints may be perfected
       And their ministry fulfilled.
    Thus we must put off the old man
       That we may put on the new;
    Thus, renewed in mind and spirit,
       We will bear God's image true.

8   Christ in love Himself has given
    That the church be sanctified,
Without blemish, spot, or wrinkle,
    To become His glorious bride.
He does nourish her and cherish
    As a man his body treats;
He and she become one Body—
    This the myst'ry very great.

9   Body, house, new man the church is,
    Bride, and temple, and yet more:
She's the army too which fighteth
    All God's foes to triumph o'er.
She is clothed with all God's armor,
    In His mighty strength is strong,
Standing in the Lord, resisting,
    With all prayers she fighteth on.

Composition for prophecy with main point and sub-points: _____

_____
_____
_____
_____
_____
_____
_____
_____
_____
_____
_____
_____
_____
_____
_____
_____
_____
_____
_____
_____
_____
_____

Growing Up into Christ in All Things and Learning Christ as the Reality Is in Jesus for the Corporate Living of the One New Man

Scripture Reading: Eph. 4:13-16, 20-21, 24

Day 1

I. **For the corporate living of the one new man, we need to grow up into Christ in all things (Eph. 4:14-16, 24):**

A. To grow up into Christ is to have Christ increase in us in all things until we arrive at a full-grown man (vv. 13-15).

B. We all need to grow up into Christ in all things, that is, in every single thing, whether big or small (v. 15):

1. There are still many things in which we have not grown up into Christ; in these things we are not in Christ but are outside of Christ.

2. When we all grow up into Christ in all things, we all will be one in Christ; this is the universal one new man (v. 24).

3. Growing up into Christ in all things is for the practical existence of the universal one new man (v. 24).

4. The growth into Christ in verse 15 equals the putting on of the new man in verse 24.

Day 2

5. The full-grown man in verse 13 refers to the one new man in verse 24, who has become full-grown.

C. Ephesians 4 speaks of the perfecting of the new man through the growth of life; the one new man created by Christ must be perfected in order to function:

1. In Ephesians 2:15 we see the creation of the new man organically; in 4:13-16 we see the perfecting of the new man in relation to his function.

2. The organically perfect one new man needs to be perfected through the growth of life in order to function in a proper way (vv. 12-15):

   a. The one new man can become perfect in relation to his function only through receiving the proper nourishment; this is one of the deepest concepts in the book of Ephesians.

   b. We need to fulfill our responsibility to perfect the one new man through nourishing and cherishing (5:29).

   c. The more the one new man grows through receiving the proper nourishment, the more he will function normally.

Day 3

3. For the growth of the corporate new man, we need to experience the crucified, resurrected, ascended, and descending Christ so that the all-inclusive Christ is wrought into us to be our everything; then the organically perfect new man will become perfect functionally (3:16-17a; 4:13, 24).

Day 4

II. **For the corporate living of the one new man, we need to learn Christ as the reality is in Jesus (vv. 20-21):**

   A. In verse 20 Paul speaks of learning Christ:

      1. Christ is not only life to us but also an example; in His life on earth the Lord Jesus set up a pattern, a mold (John 13:15; 1 Pet. 2:21).

      2. To be saved is to be put into Christ by God (1 Cor. 1:30).

      3. By means of baptism God put us into Christ, who is the pattern; to be baptized is to be placed into Christ as the mold (Rom. 6:3; Gal. 3:27).

      4. By being placed into the mold, we have put off the old man and have put on the new man (Eph. 4:22, 24).

      5. We learn Christ according to the mold of the life of Jesus, which is reality (vv. 20-21).

6. To learn Christ is to be put into Christ as the mold; it is to be molded into the pattern set up by Him during His years on earth (v. 20).

Day 5   B. The expression *the reality is in Jesus* refers to the actual condition of the life of Jesus as recorded in the four Gospels; the life of Jesus was a life of reality (v. 21):

1. In verses 17 and 21 we see a contrast between the vanity of the mind and the reality in Jesus.

2. Reality is the shining of light; light is the source, and reality is the expression (John 8:12):

   a. The Lord Jesus is the shining of God, who is light (Heb. 1:3; 1 John 1:5).

   b. Because in every aspect of the Lord's living on earth there was the shining of light, His life was a life of reality, a life of the shining God Himself; that life of reality was the expression of God (John 8:12; 14:6).

Day 6   C. The living of the one new man should be exactly the same as the living of Jesus (Eph. 4:20):

1. The way that the Lord Jesus lived on earth is the way that the new man should live today (Matt. 11:28-30; John 6:57; 4:34; 5:17, 19, 30; 6:38; 17:4).

2. Our standard of living must be according to the reality in Jesus (Eph. 4:20):

   a. He was one with God, and He lived a life in which He did everything in God, with God, and for God.

   b. The human living of Jesus was according to the reality, that is, according to God Himself, full of righteousness and holiness (v. 24).

3. We need to learn Christ and be taught in Him to live a life of reality (vv. 20-21; 2 John 1; John 4:23-24).

    4. As a corporate person, the one new man should live a life of reality, as the reality is in Jesus, which is a life of expressing God (Eph. 4:21).

    5. If we live according to the spirit of our mind, we will have the living of the corporate new man—a living that corresponds to the reality in Jesus (v. 23).

D. The church life is the daily walk of the corporate one new man, a walk that is absolutely new in nature and in manner; everything related to the one new man is new (vv. 17-32).

E. Since the one new man is according to God Himself, with God's life and nature, the one new man must have the life that is divine; such a life will be corporate, not individualistic (v. 24).

Morning Nourishment

Eph. Until we all arrive...at a full-grown man, at the meas-
4:13-15 ure of the stature of the fullness of Christ, that we
        may be no longer little children tossed by waves
        and carried about by every wind of teaching in the
        sleight of men, in craftiness with a view to a system
        of error, but holding to truth in love, we may grow
        up into Him in all things, who is the Head, Christ.

By holding to truth in love we grow up into Christ in all things. To be no longer little children (Eph. 4:14) we need to grow up into Christ. This is to have Christ increase in us in all things until we attain to a full-grown man (v. 13). The word *Head* here in verse 15 indicates that our growth in life with Christ should be the growth of the members in the Body under the Head.

To grow up into the Head means that we care only for Christ and the church. We grow by caring only for Christ and the church, that is, by handling truth in love. We do not grow by some kind of honesty or sincerity related to ethical behavior.

In verse 15 the matter of growth is specifically related to growing up into Christ, the Head, in all things. Verses 13 through 16 all point to the need for growth. If we would be a full-grown man, we need to grow. Likewise, if we would be no longer little children tossed to and fro and carried about, we also need to grow. But we should grow up into Christ not up into ourselves or into something else apart from Christ. (*Life-study of Ephesians,* p. 384)

Today's Reading

Paul clearly says that we are to grow up into the One who is the Head. This indicates that our growth must be in the Body. In order to grow into the Head, we must surely be in the Body. Many Christians are apparently growing spiritually; however, their supposed growth is not in the Body. I have known some Christians who have actually become more dissenting as they have had this kind of growth. It seems that the more they grow, the more critical they become. When they have relatively little growth, they are no problem in the church life. But as they grow, they become troublesome. This is an indication that their growth is not growth into the Head. As long as anyone's growth is not into the Head, it is not growth in the Body.... If you do not remain in the Body, you may have a certain kind of growth, but it will not be the growth into the Head.

In Ephesians 4:15 Paul tells us that we must grow up into the Head in all things. In certain aspects you have grown up into the Head, but in other aspects you probably have not.... If we bring to the Lord this matter of growing up into Him in all things, we shall see that there are many small things in which we have not yet grown up into the Head. How much we still need to grow up into Christ! May this need for growth touch our heart and turn us afresh to the Lord.

The growth into Christ in Ephesians 4:15 is equal to the putting on of the new man in verse 24. The only way to put on the new man is to grow up into Christ. The more we grow into Christ, the more we put on the new man. To put on the new man is to be in the proper church life. We cannot be in the church life if we do not grow into Christ. We need to grow up into Christ in all the details of our daily living, for example, in shopping and in talking. Often our talk is natural and devoid of Christ. The only way to be free from such a natural way of speaking is to grow out of it by growing up into Christ. If we grow in Christ in the matter of talking, our talk will eventually be in Christ. By growing up into Christ in this particular matter, we spontaneously put on more of the new man.

In order to put on the church life as the expression of the one new man, we need to grow out of everything natural by growing up into Christ. If we have the perfection with the growth spoken of in 4:13 and 15, surely we shall put on the new man. (*Life-study of Ephesians,* pp. 384-385, 674)

Further Reading: Life-study of Ephesians, msgs. 45, 80; *The Church as the Body of Christ,* ch. 15; *CWWL, 1970,* vol. 1, "The Fulfillment of God's Purpose by the Growth of Christ in Us," ch. 6

Enlightenment and inspiration: _____

_____

_____

_____

Morning Nourishment

Eph. But holding to truth in love, we may grow up into
4:15-16 Him in all things, who is the Head, Christ, out from
whom all the Body, being joined together and being knit together through every joint of the rich
supply and *through* the operation in the measure of
each one part, causes the growth of the Body unto
the building up of itself in love.

In Ephesians 2:15 Paul speaks of the creation of the one new
man: "Abolishing in His flesh the law of the commandments in
ordinances, that He might create the two in Himself into one
new man, so making peace." Then in 4:13 he speaks of arriving
at a full-grown man, and in 4:24, of putting on the new man. The
full-grown man in verse 13 is the new man in verse 24.

In 2:15 we have the creation of the new man. We may regard
this creation as the birth of the new man. Just as a child is perfected through growth, so the new man created in Christ is also
perfected through growth. This is the reason Paul refers to the
new man in chapter 4 as well as in chapter 2. (*Life-study of
Ephesians,* p. 767)

Today's Reading

We may distinguish between something that is perfect or com-
plete organically and something that is perfect according to its
function. At birth, an infant is perfect organically; that is, the infant
has all the necessary organs. However, a child is not functionally
perfect at birth....In order to develop properly and to function normally, every child needs to be nourished and cherished. This principle also applies to the church as the new man. In Ephesians 2:15
we see the creation of the new man organically, but in 4:13-16 we
see the perfecting of the new man in relation to his function.

Ephesians 4:16 is an extremely important verse....Our growth
in life is to grow into the Head, Christ, but our function in the Body
is to function out from Him. The phrase *each one part* refers to every member of the Body. Every member of the Body of Christ has

its own measure which works for the growth of the Body. The Body causes the growth of itself through the supplying joints and working parts. The growth of the Body is the increase of Christ in the church, which results in the building up of the Body itself.

In Ephesians 2 we have the birth of the new man but not the function of the new man. At birth, the new man is organically perfect; however, he is not yet able to function. Just as a child needs to be perfected through nourishing and cherishing, so the organically perfect new man needs to be perfected through the growth of life in order to function in a proper way.

Our physical life portrays this. Only God can create a being that is organically perfect....[Then] the more the child is nourished and grows, the more he will function normally.

In the same principle, the new man created by Christ must be perfected in order to function. Through the growth spoken of in chapter 4, the new man comes into function. Through the operation in the measure of each part, the Body grows unto the building up of itself in love. The creation of the new man was the responsibility of the Lord alone. We have nothing whatever to do with this. But we must fulfill our responsibility to perfect the new man through nourishing and cherishing. As the new man is perfected in this way, he grows and becomes perfect functionally.

The new man can become perfect in relation to his functions only through receiving the proper nourishment. This...is not a superficial matter. On the contrary, it is one of the deepest concepts in...Ephesians....The Body does not become functionally perfect through the teaching of doctrine. Actually, in Ephesians 4, a chapter that speaks of the perfecting of the new man through the growth of life, doctrine is depreciated. Paul says that when we are no longer children, we shall no longer be carried about by winds of teaching. What is needed for the building up of the Body and for perfecting the new man functionally is the growth of life. This comes only through feeding. (*Life-study of Ephesians,* pp. 767-769)

Further Reading: Life-study of Ephesians, msg. 92

Enlightenment and inspiration: _____

_____

_____

_____

Morning Nourishment

Eph. **For the perfecting of the saints unto the work of**
4:12-13 **the ministry, unto the building up of the Body of**
Christ, until we all arrive...at a full-grown man...
3:16-17 **That He would grant you, according to the riches of**
His glory, to be strengthened with power through
His Spirit into the inner man, that Christ may
make His home in your hearts through faith...

In today's Christianity there is not the proper function of
the members of the Body....Believers may meet together, but
they sit in their pews without functioning. The reason for this
is that...there is not the feeding that leads to genuine growth.
Only those who have been properly nourished will be able to
function.

In the Lord's recovery we need to return to what was in the
beginning. In the beginning, especially with Paul, the saints
were richly fed and nourished. If we would be perfected, what
we need is not doctrine. Rather, we need to be constituted with
Christ....We need to take Him into us more and more until we
are saturated with Him. In this way we shall become functioning members of the Body, gifts constituted by the Christ who
has been crucified and resurrected and who has ascended and
descended. (*Life-study of Ephesians,* pp. 772-773)

Today's Reading

From the time of His ascension, Christ has been working to
constitute the vanquished foes into gifts for His Body. First, He
comes to these vanquished foes and gets into them. Then He
gradually fills them and saturates them with Himself. Eventually, those who once were His enemies are transformed and constituted into useful gifts that can be presented to the Body. These
gifts will not merely teach others but will transfuse Christ into
them. In this way the members of the Body receive nourishment
and are cherished. Then they will be sanctified, purified, and
transformed to become functioning members. As a result, the
whole Body will be joined and knit together through every joint of

the rich supply and through the operation in the measure of every part. This will cause the growth of the Body unto the building up of itself in love. I believe that the day is coming when everyone in the local churches will be a functioning member.

In order for the new man to grow, we need to experience the crucified, resurrected, ascended, and descending Christ. This means that the all-inclusive Christ must be wrought into us to be our everything. Then the organically perfect new man will also become perfect functionally.

The new man is not perfected mainly by teaching. Teaching may actually be a frustration to our growth in life. Before the new man could be created, all the ordinances had to be abolished....Ordinances are obstacles to the formation of the new man, and doctrines are frustrations to the growth of the new man....Growth only comes through the experience of Christ. The degree to which we can minister Christ is in direct proportion to our experience of Christ....As we minister Christ, others will be nourished.

The very Christ who was crucified and resurrected and who has ascended to the third heaven is now working within us to constitute us into functioning members of the Body. He carries out this work by making His home in our hearts and by saturating us with Himself. As He saturates us, we are sanctified, purified, nourished, cherished, and transformed. The result is that we become perfected functionally. In this way the Body grows and builds itself up. The Body is not built directly by the Head or by the gifts mentioned in Ephesians 4:11; it is built up directly by those members who have been perfected by the gifted ones.

The more we are saturated with Christ, the more we become in reality parts of the Body with a particular measure of function. Then wherever we may be we shall function properly, and the Body will grow. This will cause Satan, the enemy of God, to tremble. It will also hasten the coming back of the Lord Jesus. (*Life-study of Ephesians,* pp. 773, 775-776)

Further Reading: Life-study of Ephesians, msg. 93

Enlightenment and inspiration: _____

_____

_____

_____

Morning Nourishment

Eph. **But you did not so learn Christ, if indeed you have**
4:20-21 **heard Him and have been taught in Him as the**
reality is in Jesus.

Ephesians 4:17 through 19 is a dark background for what
Paul says in verse 20, "But you did not so learn Christ." The New
Testament strongly indicates that we should live Christ. In Philippians 1:21 Paul declares, "To me, to live is Christ." But here in
Ephesians 4:20 we are told that we have learned Christ. Notice
that Paul uses the past tense in speaking of our learning Christ.
He also uses the past tense in the next verse, which says, "If
indeed you have heard Him and have been taught in Him as the
reality is in Jesus." (*Life-study of Ephesians,* pp. 392-393)

Today's Reading

Christ is not only life to us but also an example (John 13:15;
1 Pet. 2:21). We learn from Him (Matt. 11:29) according to His example, not by our natural life but by Him as our life. According to
the New Testament, the Lord Jesus did not come into us as life directly. Rather, after living on earth for thirty years, He ministered
for another three and a half years. During the thirty-three and a
half years of His life on earth, He set up a pattern, a mold, a model.
This is a matter of great significance. One reason the four Gospels
were written was to show the pattern of the life that God desires,
the mold of the life that can satisfy God and fulfill His purpose. For
this reason, the New Testament gives us a unique biography, the
biography of the Lord Jesus, written from four directions. After the
Lord Jesus set up the pattern revealed in the Gospels, He was crucified on the cross and then He entered into resurrection. It is in
resurrection that He comes into us to be our life.

According to the New Testament, to be saved is to be put by
God into Christ [cf. 1 Cor. 1:30]....When God put us into Christ, He
put us into the mold....God intends to form us into the mold of
Christ. Hence, Romans 8:29 indicates that we are to be conformed
to the image of Christ, the Firstborn among many brothers. To be
conformed is to be molded. The Firstborn is the pattern, and the

many brothers of the Firstborn are those who are to be conformed to this pattern. To learn Christ is simply to be molded into the pattern of Christ, that is, to be conformed to the image of Christ.

By means of baptism God has put us into Christ, who is the pattern. To be baptized is to be placed into Christ as the mold. Both Romans 6:3 and Galatians 3:27 speak of being baptized into Christ. To be baptized into Christ is to be buried into Him. The tomb of this baptism is the pattern, the mold....Through being placed into the mold, we have put off the old man and have put on the new man. By being buried into Christ, we have been brought out of Adam and the old creation. By baptism we have been put into Christ, who is both our life and our pattern. This explains why Paul uses the past tense in speaking about learning Christ. We learned Christ when we were buried into Him in baptism. This means that to learn Christ is to be put into Christ as the mold. It is to be molded into the pattern set up by Him during His years on earth.

After Christ established the pattern, He was crucified, and then He entered into resurrection, becoming in resurrection the life-giving Spirit (1 Cor. 15:45). It is as the Spirit that He comes into us to be our life. We have pointed out that at the time we believed in Christ and were baptized in Him, God put us into Him as the pattern, the mold. Therefore, Paul could tell the Ephesians that they "did...learn Christ." According to the light of the New Testament and according to our experience, to learn Christ is to be placed into Christ by God. On God's side, He has put us into Christ. On our side, we have learned Christ by being put into Him.

After a person is saved,...he desires to live a life in the pattern established by the Lord Jesus. However, many either ignore this desire or cultivate it in a mistaken way, thinking that by self-effort they can succeed in imitating Him. It is a mistake to think that we can imitate Christ by the exercise of our natural life. The believers in Christ should imitate Him, but they should not do so according to their natural life. (*Life-study of Ephesians,* pp. 393-394)

Further Reading: Life-study of Ephesians, msgs. 46, 49

Enlightenment and inspiration: _____

_____

_____

_____

Morning Nourishment

Eph. This therefore I say and testify in the Lord, that
4:17 you no longer walk as the Gentiles also walk in the
      vanity of their mind.
20-21 But you did not so learn Christ, if indeed you have
       heard Him and have been taught in Him as the
       reality is in Jesus.

The truth [reality] in Jesus is the real situation of the life of
Jesus as recorded in the four Gospels. In the godless walk of the
nations, the fallen people, there is vanity. But in the godly life
of Jesus there is truth, reality. Jesus lived a life always doing
things in God, with God, and for God. God was in His life, and
He was one with God. This is the reality in Jesus. We, the
believers, regenerated with Christ as our life and taught in
Him, learn from Him as the reality is in Jesus. (*Life-study of
Ephesians,* pp. 394-395)

Today's Reading

It is a mistake to endeavor to imitate Christ by the efforts of
our natural life....When we believed in the Lord Jesus and were
saved, God put us into Christ as the mold. This mold is the life
of Jesus recorded in the four Gospels, a life absolutely according to truth. Truth is the shining of light, the expression of
light. Since God is light (1 John 1:5), truth is the expression
of God. Every aspect of the life of Jesus recorded in the Gospels
is an expression of God. In everything He said and did, He
expressed God. This expression of God is the shining of light;
hence, it is the truth. This life of Jesus according to truth is the
pattern in which God has placed us....This life is the shining of
light. The shining of the light is truth, and truth is the expression of God. Therefore, in the life of Jesus there is truth. The
essence of the pattern set up by the Lord Jesus is truth. This
means that the essence of the life of Jesus is truth, reality. We
have learned Christ as the reality is in Jesus.

The truth, the reality, in Jesus in Ephesians 4:21 is in contrast to the vanity of the mind in verse 17. The nations walk in

the vanity of their mind, but we believers live a life as the truth is in Jesus. When the Lord Jesus was living on earth, He never walked in vanity. Rather, He always walked in truth, that is, in the shining of the divine light. This means that the Lord Jesus lived and walked in the expression of God. We have learned Christ according to this very truth that is in Jesus. (*Life-study of Ephesians,* p. 395)

In His thirty-three and a half years on earth, the Lord Jesus formed the mold, the pattern, to which all those who believe in Him are to be conformed. According to the record of the four Gospels, the life of the Lord Jesus was a life of reality. Reality is the shining of light. Light is the source, and reality is its expression. As Hebrews 1:3 says, the Lord Jesus is the effulgence of God's glory. This means that He is the shining of God who is light. Because in every aspect of the Lord's living on earth there was the shining of light, His life was a life of reality, a life of the shining of God Himself. That life of reality was the expression of God. For this reason Paul says that we learn Christ as the reality is in Jesus. In other words, we learn Christ according to the mold of the life of Jesus, which is the reality.

After Christ established this mold, He passed through death and resurrection, and in resurrection He became the life-giving Spirit. As such a Spirit, He comes into us to be our life. When we believed in Christ and were baptized, God put us into Him as the mold, just as dough is placed into a mold. By being put into the mold, we learn the mold. This means that by being put into Christ, we learn Christ. On the one hand, God put us into Christ; on the other hand, Christ has come into us to be our life. Now we may live by Him according to the mold in which we have been placed by God. We are in Christ as the mold, and He is in us as our life. In this way we learn Christ as the reality is in Jesus. (*The Conclusion of the New Testament,* pp. 3427-3428)

Further Reading: The Conclusion of the New Testament, msg. 341; *The Believer's Experience of Transformation,* ch. 4

Enlightenment and inspiration: _____

_____

_____

_____

Morning Nourishment

John
6:57   As the living Father has sent Me and I live because of the Father, so he who eats Me, he also shall live because of Me.

Eph.
4:22-24   That you put off, as regards your former manner of life, the old man, which is being corrupted according to the lusts of the deceit, and *that* you be renewed in the spirit of your mind and put on the new man, which was created according to God in righteousness and holiness of the reality.

Paul speaks of learning Christ (Eph. 4:20) and of having been "taught in Him as the reality is in Jesus" (v. 21)....The reality, the truth, in Jesus is the real situation of the life of Jesus as recorded in the four Gospels, a life filled with truth, reality....Jesus lived in a way that always corresponded to God's righteousness and holiness.

In verse 24 Paul says that the new man "was created according to God in righteousness and holiness of the reality." This reality no doubt is the very reality in Jesus. Our standard of living should not be according to the law or according to the standards of society; it must be according to the truth in Jesus, the reality lived out by Jesus when He was on earth. Hence, the life of Jesus should be our life today in the church. In other words, the living of the new man should be exactly the same as the living of Jesus. The way Jesus lived on earth is the way the new man should live today. (*Life-study of Ephesians,* pp. 780-781)

Today's Reading

If we would live in such a way, we should not reason according to right or wrong. Instead, we should consider the various aspects of our daily life according to the truth as it is in Jesus. For example, if we are about to go shopping, we should ask whether the Lord Jesus is going shopping. The life of the one new man must be that of the reality of Jesus. If we all live in a way that is heavenly, divine, righteous, holy, and glorious, we shall have a wonderful community life in the church. This is the corporate life of the new man.

The key to the church life is the spirit of the mind. If we live according to the spirit of the mind, there will be in the church life the expression of the divine character. Then we shall be a corporate people with the flavor of Christ and the expression of God. If we simply give others the impression that we are good, righteous, and kind, our church life is a failure. There must be in our goodness, righteousness, and kindness the expression of the Triune God. The church life must be filled with the aroma and flavor of Christ and with the character of God. Such a living is the living of the Triune God through our humanity. For centuries, God has been longing for such a church life.

In the church as the new man, we should live not according to the vanity of the mind, but according to the spirit of the mind (Eph. 4:23). This is the key to the daily living of the corporate one new man. Formerly, our mind was filled with vanity; now it must be permeated with the spirit. We need to walk according to the spirit that is spreading into our mind and filling it. In this way the daily walk of the new man will be in the spirit of the mind. This is the secret of the church life.

In verse 24 Paul says that the new man is according to God. This means that the new man is according to God Himself, with God's life and nature. Since the new man is according to God, it must have a life that is divine. Such a life will not be individualistic; it will be corporate.

We do not have the church life simply by coming together in the meetings to sing, pray-read, praise the Lord, and give testimonies. The church life is the daily walk of a corporate man, a walk that is absolutely new in nature and in manner. If we walk according to the spirit of our mind, we shall be those who live such a corporate life. We shall have the proper community life in which everything is new. May the Lord hasten the day when concerning this matter our sky is clear and we are fully in the light! (*Life-study of Ephesians*, pp. 781, 792, 783-784, 779)

Further Reading: Life-study of Ephesians, msg. 94

Enlightenment and inspiration: _____

_____

_____

_____

Hymns, #1325

1   God eternal has a purpose,
    Formed in His eternal past,
    Spreading to eternal future;
    'Twixt these ends all time is cast.
    For with time there is the process,
    Time for His accomplishment;
    And in time we're merely travelers—
    For eternity we're meant.

2   God would have a group of people
    Built together in His plan,
    Blended, knit, coordinated
    As His vessel—one new man.
    God would come into this vessel
    With His nature, life and ways,
    Mingling Spirit with our spirits
    For His joy and to His praise.

3   God has worked in three directions
    For His plan so marvelous:
    As the Father, Son, and Spirit
    To dispense Himself to us!
    All creation gives the setting—
    Heav'n and earth are for this plan;
    'Tis for this God made a body,
    Soul, and spirit—three-part man.

4   As the center, as the kernel,
    Of God's plan our spirit is;
    Calling on the name of Jesus
    Makes our spirit one with His.
    From the center to circumf'rence
    God would saturate each part;
    Feeling, mind, and will renewing,
    Making home in all our heart.

5   Thus in life we're built together,
    Then in love we're knit as one;
    God is now His plan fulfilling,
    Finishing what He's begun.
    Lord, increase Thyself within us
    That we might be built by Thee
    Into that great corporate vessel
    Filled with God exclusively.

6   As the product, the fulfillment,
    Will the church in glory stand,
    Consummation of the purpose
    In eternal ages planned.
    God will have His corporate vessel,
    All His glory to contain;
    Lord, we're wholly for Thy purpose,
    All Thy goal in us attain.

Composition for prophecy with main point and sub-points: _____

_____
_____
_____
_____
_____
_____
_____
_____
_____
_____
_____
_____
_____
_____
_____
_____
_____
_____
_____
_____
_____
_____
_____
_____
_____
_____

Experiencing Christ
as Our Life, Our Person,
for the One New Man

Scripture Reading: Col. 3:1-4, 10-11

Day 1

I. **In order to experience Christ as our life, our person, we need to see that we have one position, one life, one living, one destiny, and one glory with Christ (Col. 3:1-4; cf. 1 Cor. 6:17):**

A. Our position is that we are in Christ; because we are in Him, we are where He is—sitting at the right hand of God (Col. 3:1; John 17:24; Eph. 2:6):

1. The Son's position is in the Father (John 10:38; 14:10); we are in the Son (1 Cor. 1:30a), so we are in the Father (John 14:20; 1 Thes. 1:1; 2 Thes. 1:1).

2. It is when we are in the spirit that we are in Christ, in the Father, and in heaven practically and experientially:

a. There is a transmission taking place from Christ in heaven to us on earth by means of the all-inclusive Spirit in our spirit (Eph. 1:19, 22-23; 2:22).

b. The very Christ who is sitting on the throne in heaven (Rom. 8:34) is also now in us (v. 10), that is, in our spirit (2 Tim. 4:22), where the habitation of God is (Eph. 2:22).

c. Since today our spirit is the place of God's habitation, it is now the gate of heaven, where Christ is the ladder that joins us to heaven and brings heaven to us (v. 22; Gen. 28:12-17; John 1:51).

d. Whenever we turn to our spirit, we enter through the gate of heaven and touch the throne of grace in heaven through Christ as the heavenly ladder; our spirit is the receiving end of the divine transmission, whereas the throne of God is the transmitting end (Heb. 4:16).

Day 2

B. The life of God is the life of Christ, and the life of Christ has become our life (John 5:26; Col. 3:4):

   1. For Christ to be our life means that He is subjective to us to the uttermost (John 1:4; 14:6a; 10:10b; 1 Cor. 15:45b; Rom. 8:10, 6, 11).

   2. It is impossible to separate a person from the life of that person, for a person's life is the person himself; thus, to say that Christ is our life means that Christ has become us and that we have one life and living with Him (John 14:6a; Phil. 1:21a).

   3. With Christ as the believers' life, there are three characteristics that distinguish this life from the natural life:

      a. This life is a crucified life (Gal. 2:20).

      b. This life is a resurrected life (John 11:25).

      c. This is a life hidden in God (Col. 3:3-4; Matt. 6:1-6, 16-18).

Day 3

C. To seek the things which are above and set our mind on them is to join ourselves to the Lord in His heavenly ministry, His divine enterprise; this is to live Christ, to have a living that is one with Christ's living for the one new man (Col. 3:1-2, 10-11):

   1. In His heavenly ministry Christ today is living as the High Priest to intercede for the churches (Heb. 8:1; 4:14; 7:25; 4:16; Col. 4:2).

   2. In His heavenly ministry Christ today is living as the heavenly Minister to supply the saints with the riches of Christ (Heb. 8:1-2; Eph. 3:8).

   3. In His heavenly ministry Christ today is living as the universal Administrator of God's government for the accomplishment of God's purpose (Rev. 4:1-2, 5; 5:6; 1:10-11):

      a. From the throne in the heavens, the divine transmission brings the things

above into the local churches (Eph. 1:19,
22-23).

b. In Revelation 4 and 5 we have a vision
of our central government, and in Revelation 1 through 3 we have a vision of
the local churches as the "embassies";
through the seven Spirits what is in the
heavenly headquarters is transmitted
into the churches as the embassies.

c. What takes place in the local churches
should be under the direction of the throne
of God in heaven; in order for the recovery to be the *Lord's* recovery, it must be
under His direction (Col. 1:18; 2:19; Rev.
4:2-3).

Day 4   D. Our destiny is glory; Christ is leading us into
glory for us to be manifested with Him in glory
(Heb. 2:10; Col. 3:4).

II. Our life is the Christ who dwells within us,
and this life is hidden with Christ in God;
the Christ hidden in God is typified by the
manna hidden in the golden pot (vv. 3-4; Exo.
16:32-34; Rev. 2:17):

A. Christ as the hidden manna is in God the Father
as the golden pot; the Father is in Christ as the
Ark with His two natures, divinity and humanity; and Christ as the indwelling Spirit lives in
our regenerated spirit to be the reality of the
Holy of Holies (cf. John 14:16-20; 2 Tim. 4:22).

B. When we eat Christ as the hidden manna, we are
incorporated into Him for the mutual abode of
God and man (John 15:5, 7; 8:31; 6:57, 63; 14:23).

Day 5 III. That Christ is our life is a strong indication
that we are to take Him as life and live by
Him, that we are to live Him in our daily life
(Col. 3:4a):

A. Christ must be our life in a practical and experiential way; day by day we need to be saved in His
life (v. 4a; 1 Cor. 15:45b; Rom. 5:10):

1. To be saved in the divine life from the slavery of sin, the law of sin, is by the release of the law of the consummated Spirit (8:2).
2. To be saved in the divine life from the present age of the world is by the sanctification of the consummated Spirit (12:2a; 6:19b, 22b).
3. To be saved in the divine life from our natural being is by the transformation of the life-giving Spirit (12:2b).
4. To be saved in the divine life from individualism is by being built up in the Body of Christ (v. 5).

Day 6

5. To be saved in the divine life from self-likeness is by the conformation of the life-imparting Spirit (8:29).
6. To be saved in the divine life from our body of humiliation is by the transfiguration in the virtue of the divine life (v. 30; Phil. 3:21; Rom. 8:11).
7. To be saved in the divine life is to reign in the divine life (5:17).
8. To be saved in the divine life will result in the victory over Satan (16:20).

B. The new man is the spontaneous issue of our taking Christ as our life and living Him (Col. 3:3-4, 10-11).

Morning Nourishment

Col. **If therefore you were raised together with Christ,**
3:1-2 **seek the things which are above, where Christ is,**
    sitting at the right hand of God. Set your mind on
    the things which are above, not on the things which
    are on the earth.

Colossians 3:1-4 implies that with Christ we have one position, one life, one living, one destiny, and one glory. Because we and Christ have one position, we are where He is. We and Christ also have one life, even the same life. The life He has we have also. Moreover, we have one living with Christ. Our living is His living. When we live, He lives, for He lives in our living. If we have one living with Christ in a practical way day by day, then whatever we do, He does also. This means that when we talk, He talks....[However], if we become angry and Christ is not angry, we do not have one living with Him at that particular time. In such a case, our living is not His living.

We also have one glory and destiny with Christ. Glory is our future and our destination. The Lord Jesus is now in glory. However, He is in glory in a way that is hidden from mankind....One day Christ will be in glory no longer in a hidden way, but in an open way, in the way of manifestation. Then everyone on earth will know that the Lord Jesus is in glory....This is our destiny as well. (*Life-study of Colossians,* pp. 517-518)

Today's Reading

Our position is that we are in Christ. Because we are in Him, we are where He is—at the right hand of God (Col. 3:1). In John 17:24 the Lord Jesus prayed, "Father, concerning that which You have given Me, I desire that they also may be with Me where I am."...Our position is not only in Christ but also in the Father. In the Gospel of John we are told clearly that the Son is in the Father (10:38; 14:10). This means that the Son's position is in the Father. Since our position today is that we are in the Son, in Christ, we also are in the Father. The Father, of course, is in heaven. Hence, our position also is that we are in heaven....What makes this real is that we are one spirit with the Lord (1 Cor. 6:17). It is when we are in the spirit that we are in Christ, in the Father, and in heaven practically and experientially.

A transmission is going on from heaven to our spirit! When we experience this transmission, we are truly in Christ, in the Father, and in heaven. Our spirit is directly related to heaven. The heavenly transmission begins in heaven and ends in our spirit.

There is a transmission taking place from Christ in heaven to us on earth by means of the all-inclusive Spirit....Hallelujah for the transmission from the third heaven into us! "There's a Man in the glory / Whose Life is for me" (*Hymns,* #505). Christ is the Man in the glory, but His life is for us. We all need a vision of the heavenly transmission from the glorified Christ into us. Furthermore, we need to stay open to this transmission so that it will not be cut off....May there be no insulation to hinder this divine transmission.

Our spirit is the receiving end of the divine transmission, whereas the throne of God in heaven is the transmitting end. Thus, by turning to our spirit, we are lifted into heaven. Then in our experience we are in Christ, in the Father, and in heaven. Then in the spirit we are one in position with Christ, seeking the things which are above. (*Life-study of Colossians,* pp. 518-519, 509-510, 520)

The very Christ who is sitting on the throne in heaven (Rom. 8:34) is also now in us (Rom. 8:10), that is, in our spirit (2 Tim. 4:22), where the habitation of God is (Eph. 2:22). At Bethel, the house of God, the habitation of God, which is the gate of heaven, Christ is the ladder that joins earth to heaven and brings heaven to earth (Gen. 28:12-17; John 1:51). Since today our spirit is the place of God's habitation, it is now the gate of heaven, where Christ is the ladder that joins us, the people on earth, to heaven, and brings heaven to us. Hence, whenever we turn to our spirit, we enter through the gate of heaven and touch the throne of grace in heaven through Christ as the heavenly ladder. (Heb. 4:16, footnote 1)

Further Reading: Life-study of Colossians, msg. 59

Enlightenment and inspiration: _____

_____

_____

_____

Morning Nourishment

Col. For you died, and your life is hidden with Christ in
3:3-4 God. When Christ our life is manifested, then you
also will be manifested with Him in glory.

In Colossians 3:3 and 4 Paul twice speaks of life, indicating
thereby that we have one life with Christ. In verse 3 he says
that our life "is hidden with Christ in God." In verse 4 he goes
on to speak of when "Christ our life is manifested."

According to our experience and according to the Word, life
here is Christ's life becoming our life. If it were merely Christ's
life, it could not be called "our life." The very fact that it is "our
life" indicates that it refers to something which has become
ours. However, the life here is not our natural life, the life inherited from Adam. Such a life could never be that which is hidden
with Christ in God. God would never allow the natural life
inherited from Adam to be hidden in Him. The only life that
can be hidden with Christ in God is the divine life, the very life
of Christ. It is this life which has become our life. Paul's use of
the expression "our life" indicates that we and Christ, and also
God Himself, have one life. We should not think that God has
one life, that Christ has another life, and that we who believe
in Christ have yet another life. Rather, God, Christ, and the
believers have one life. The life of God is the life of Christ, and
the life of Christ has become our life.

We see a sister who is gentle, quiet, and kind, and we think
that because she has such characteristics she is full of life.
Seeing a brother who is an eloquent and powerful speaker, we
may take his power and eloquence as signs of life. However, in
both cases what we see may be the natural life, not the life that
Christ has, the life hidden with Christ in God. (*Life-study of
Colossians*, pp. 520-521)

Today's Reading

Colossians 3:4 speaks of "Christ our life." Christ is God and
also life (1 John 5:12). The life which is God, the life that God is, is
in Christ (John 1:4). Hence, the Lord Jesus said that He is life

(John 14:6; 11:25) and that He came that we may have life (John 10:10). Therefore, he who has Christ has life (1 John 5:12), and He now dwells in the believers as life. Just as life is God Himself, so also life is Christ. Just as having life is having God Himself, so also having life is having Christ. Christ is God becoming life to us. Through Christ God is manifested as life. Therefore, Christ is now our life.

Christ must be our life in a practical and experiential way day by day. He should be our life within, and we should have one life and living with Him.

For Christ to be our life means that He is subjective to us to the uttermost. Nothing is more subjective to us, or more intimately related to us, than our life. Our life is actually we ourselves. It is impossible to separate a person from the life of that person, for a person's life is the person himself. If we did not have life, we would cease to be. To say that Christ has become our life means that Christ has become us. Since our life cannot be separated from us and since Christ is our life, He cannot be separated from us. Because our life is our self and because Christ is our life, we may say that, in this sense, Christ has become us.

With Christ as the believers' life there are three characteristics. First, this life is a crucified life. When the Lord Jesus was on earth, He always lived a crucified life. If we truly experience Christ as our life, we also shall live a crucified life. Such a crucified life is a life that has been processed and thoroughly dealt with. The second characteristic of Christ as our life is that this life is a resurrected life. Nothing, including death, can suppress it. Finally, this is a life hidden in God (Col. 3:3). Only the divine life can be hidden in God. If we experience Christ as our life, what we do in the church will not be done in a showy way but rather be done by a life hidden in God. (*The Conclusion of the New Testament*, pp. 543-545)

Further Reading: The Conclusion of the New Testament, msg. 50

Enlightenment and inspiration: _____

_____

_____

_____

Morning Nourishment

Heb. ...We have such a High Priest, who sat down on the
8:1   right hand of the throne of the Majesty in the heavens.
7:25 Hence also He is able to save to the uttermost those
        who come forward to God through Him, since He
        lives always to intercede for them.
Col.   Persevere in prayer, watching in it with thanks-
4:2   giving.

To seek the things which are above and to set our mind on
them is to join ourselves to the Lord in His ministry in heaven.
We need to join ourselves to the very One who is interceding,
ministering, and executing God's administration. Our living
should be a kind of living in which we seek these heavenly
things and set our mind on them. This means that we live in
such a way as to join our heavenly Christ in His priesthood,
ministry, and administration.

We are not here to seek earthly things but to have a living
that is one with Christ's living. Christ today is living as the
High Priest, the heavenly Minister, and the universal Administrator. We need to join Him in His living and have one living
with Him. (*Life-study of Colossians*, pp. 524-525)

Today's Reading

Christ in heaven is very active, even more busy than when
He was on earth. He is interceding for us, shepherding all His
churches, and ministering on behalf of millions of saints. As the
High Priest in heaven, He is interceding for us....As He inter-
cedes for us, Christ is ministering the heavenly life supply into
us. He is the heavenly Minister ministering in the heavens (Heb.
8:1-2). According to Revelation 5:6, as the Lamb on the throne,
Christ is executing God's universal administration. Because Christ
is so active for us in the heavens, we should seek the things that
are above and set our mind on them.

To seek the things above and to set our mind on them is to live
Christ, to have one living with Him. When Christ prays in heaven,
we should pray on earth. This means that there is a transmission

between the Christ praying in heaven and us praying on earth. By means of this transmission we may pray in oneness with Him.

Christ today is living in the heavens to intercede for the churches, to minister the heavenly life supply to the saints, and to carry out God's administration....We thank the Lord that a number of those in the local churches today..., when they sense that Christ is praying in heaven for a certain matter,...join Him to pray on earth for that very matter....To pray together with Christ in this way is to have one living with Him.

In the book of Revelation we see even more of the things which are above....Heaven was opened to John, and he saw "a throne set in heaven, and upon the throne there was One sitting" (Rev. 4:1-2). This throne is not simply the throne of grace, but is the very throne of authority, the throne of the divine administration.

The first vision [in the book of Revelation] is of the churches on earth [1:12, 20], whereas the second vision is of what is taking place in the heavens. When considered together, these two visions indicate that what is happening in the churches on earth is related to the activity in the heavens....The Lord's move in the churches corresponds to the action on the throne in heaven. This means that what takes place in the local churches should be under the direction of the throne of God in heaven. In order for the recovery to be the *Lord's* recovery, it must be under His direction. As long as there is a transmission coming from the heavens, there will be the divine flow in the churches.

In Revelation 4 and 5 we have a vision of our central government, and in Revelation 1 through 3 we have a vision of the local churches as the "embassies." Through the seven Spirits there is a transmission going on from the heavenly headquarters into the embassies. Through the seven Spirits what is in the headquarters is transmitted into the churches....From the throne in the heavens, the divine transmission brings the things above into the local churches. (*Life-study of Colossians,* pp. 531-533, 513-515)

Further Reading: Life-study of Colossians, msgs. 58, 60

Enlightenment and inspiration: _____

_____

_____

_____

Morning Nourishment

Heb. For it was fitting for Him,...in leading many sons
2:10 into glory, to make the Author of their salvation
      perfect through sufferings.
Rev. He who has an ear, let him hear what the Spirit says
2:17 to the churches. To him who overcomes, to him I will
      give of the hidden manna, and to him I will give a
      white stone, and upon the stone a new name written,
      which no one knows except him who receives *it.*

Our destiny is glory. Today we are hidden in God, but when
Christ is manifested, we shall be manifested with Him in glory
(Col. 3:4). When we are manifested with Christ, we shall be on
display to the whole universe....However, today we should not
make a show, but should remain hidden in God, waiting for the
time when we shall arrive at our destination and enter into
glory with Christ. Then, at the appointed time, the time for a
divinely-ordained display, there will be the manifestation of
the sons of God in glory. (*Life-study of Colossians,* p. 526)

Today's Reading

In Exodus 16:33 we see that an omer full of manna was
placed in a pot and laid up before the Lord to be kept for future
generations. Hebrews 9:4 speaks of "the golden pot that had
the manna." Thus, the hidden manna was in a golden pot. The
manna concealed in the golden pot signifies that our life is
hidden with Christ in God [cf. Col. 3:3]....The Christ hidden in
God is the manna hidden in the golden pot.

In the Bible gold signifies the divine nature. According to 2 Peter 1:4, we are partakers of this divine nature. Only the nature of
God, the divine nature, can preserve Christ as our hidden manna.
Praise the Lord that within us we have a golden pot; that is, we
have the divine nature. We cannot preserve Christ in our mind or
emotion. We can preserve Him only in the divine nature which we
have within us through regeneration. Actually, the divine nature
within us is God Himself. The manna in the golden pot indicates
that the very Christ whom we enjoy as our life supply is preserved

in the divine nature which is now in our inmost being. Christ is our special portion of food hidden in the divine nature. When we touch the divine nature, the golden pot, we enjoy Christ as the manna hidden within it. (*Life-study of Exodus,* p. 455)

The tabernacle in the Old Testament is a sign of the universal incorporation. Christ as the hidden manna is the center of the tabernacle. The hidden manna is in the golden pot; the golden pot is in the Ark, made of acacia wood overlaid with gold; and this Ark is in the Holy of Holies. The hidden manna, which signifies Christ, is in the golden pot, which refers to God. The manna in the golden pot indicates that Christ is in the Father (John 14:10a, 11a). The Ark is in the Holy of Holies, and the Holy of Holies is our spirit. Today, our spirit indwelt by the Holy Spirit is the Holy of Holies. From this we can see that Christ as the hidden manna is in God the Father as the golden pot; that the Father is in Christ as the Ark with His two natures, divinity and humanity; and that this Christ as the indwelling Spirit lives in our regenerated spirit to be the reality of the Holy of Holies. This means that the Son is in the Father, that the Father is in the Son, and that the Son as the Spirit is the reality of the Holy of Holies. This implies and corresponds to the four *in*s in John 14:16-20. Verse 20 says, "In that day you will know that I am in My Father, and you in Me, and I in you," and verse 17 says, "The Spirit of reality...shall be in you." The Son is in the Father, we are in the Son, the Son is in us, and we are indwelt by the Spirit of reality. This is the incorporation of the processed God with the regenerated believers.

The way to be incorporated into the tabernacle is to eat the hidden manna. The more we eat Christ, the more we are incorporated into the Triune God as a universal incorporation. By eating the hidden manna we are incorporated into the tabernacle. (*The Issue of Christ Being Glorified by the Father with the Divine Glory,* pp. 30-31)

Further Reading: Life-study of Exodus, msg. 39; *The Issue of Christ Being Glorified by the Father with the Divine Glory,* ch. 4*

Enlightenment and inspiration: _____

_____

_____

_____

Morning Nourishment

Rom. For if we, being enemies, were reconciled to God
5:10 through the death of His Son, much more we will
be saved in His life, having been reconciled.
12:2 And do not be fashioned according to this age, but
be transformed by the renewing of the mind that
you may prove what the will of God is...
5 So we who are many are one Body in Christ, and
individually members one of another.

In salvation Christ is not only our objective Savior; He is also
our subjective life. In Colossians 3:4 Paul speaks of "Christ our
life." The expression "our life" is a strong indication that we need
to experience Christ in our daily living. Christ, not our self, our
soul, should be our life.

[Romans 5:10] covers both the reconciling death of Christ and
the saving life of Christ. Reconciliation includes redemption and
justification. Christ died on the cross for our redemption. Through
redemption we have been justified by God and reconciled to Him.
Now there is nothing between us and God. However, we still have
a number of subjective problems. For this reason, even after we
have been reconciled to God, we still need to be saved in Christ's
life. (*The Conclusion of the New Testament,* p. 312)

Today's Reading

We, as God's redeemed people, are saved in the divine life of
Christ by the release of the law of the consummated Spirit from
the bondage, the slavery, of sin, the law of sin (Rom. 8:2). The law
of the consummated Spirit is the means for the release from the
bondage of sin....But in order for the law of the consummated
Spirit to operate, there is the need of our cooperation by setting
our mind on the mingled spirit (v. 6b) and by walking according
to the mingled spirit (v. 4).

We also need to be saved in the divine life of Christ by the
sanctification of the consummated Spirit from the present age
of the world (12:2a; 6:19b, 22b)....Through incarnation, death,
and resurrection, the Spirit of God became equipped and

qualified to impart life to man and to save man in the divine life.

We need to be sanctified by the consummated Spirit, not by our strong will or mind, from the present age of this world. I may read the newspaper in order to realize something concerning the world situation…, [but] I do not want to be modern or to be conformed to the modern age. Rather, I want to be transformed by the Spirit.

We are saved in the divine life of Christ from our natural being by the transformation of the life-giving Spirit (12:2b). Transformation is not merely a change in outward appearance. Transformation is an inward, metabolic change, which involves something organic.

Transformation is by the renewing of our mind (v. 2b). Formerly, our mind was set on the flesh. Now, we must change the position of our mind by setting it on the spirit. The mind set on the spirit is life and peace (8:6). Changing the position of our mind will transform our mind.

We are transformed by the metabolism in the element of the divine life (Col. 3:4). Christ is our life. In any kind of organic life there is an organic element. Christ is the organic element that grows within us and transforms us.

We are saved in the divine life of Christ from individualism by being built in the Body of Christ (Rom. 12:5). Today on the earth there are very few Christians who have been built into the Body of Christ. All of us are still on the way of being built in the Body of Christ. We are still too individualistic. There is a certain percentage of individualism that still remains in us.

We are built in the Body of Christ and saved from individualism by presenting our bodies a living sacrifice (v. 1) and by not thinking more highly of ourselves than what we are (v. 3).…Most of the troubles in the church life mainly come from thinking more highly of ourselves than what we are. (*CWWL, 1990,* vol. 1, "The Triune God to Be Life to the Tripartite Man," pp. 284-287)

Further Reading: The Conclusion of the New Testament, msg. 29

Enlightenment and inspiration: _____

_____

_____

_____

Morning Nourishment

Rom.   Because those whom He foreknew, He also predesti-
8:29-30 nated *to be* conformed to the image of His Son…; and
those whom He predestinated, these He also called;
and those whom He called, these He also justified;
and those whom He justified, these He also glorified.

Col.   And have put on the new man, which is being re-
3:10-11 newed unto full knowledge according to the image of
Him who created him, where…Christ is all and in all.

We are saved in the divine life of Christ from self-likeness by
the conformation of the life-imparting Spirit (Rom. 8:29b). This is
another aspect of the Spirit. Whether we are bad or good, nice or
rough, we still bear our self-likeness. Therefore, we need conformation through transformation into the very image of the Son of
God. This conformation is for the maturity in the divine life.

The issue of our being saved in the divine life of Christ is transfiguration, in the virtue of the divine life, from our body of humiliation (v. 30c; Phil. 3:21; Rom. 8:11). The transfiguration of our body is
the redemption of our body through the indwelling Spirit. When
the indwelling Spirit saturates us thoroughly, our body will be redeemed. The saturation of our body with the Spirit will be the
transfiguration of our body.…The transfiguration from our body of
humiliation is by the redeeming of our body through the indwelling
Spirit as the firstfruits, the foretaste (v. 23). (*CWWL, 1990,* vol. 1,
"The Triune God to Be Life to the Tripartite Man," pp. 287-288)

Today's Reading

When we are saved in the divine life by being released, sanctified, transformed, conformed, and transfigured, we can reign in
the divine life (Rom. 5:17). The more we live and are saved in the
divine life, the more we exercise the kingship and reign in the divine life. The divine life is kingly and royal. The overcomers will
be co-kings with Christ in the millennium (Rev. 20:4, 6) because
they will be saturated and swallowed up by the divine life. Because they are full of life, they become the embodiment of life, and
they will also have the kingship in full. They reign because they

are full of life. The matter of reigning in the divine life is referred to by John (Rev. 20:4, 6) and is also one of the particular items stressed in Paul's writings (Rom. 5:17; 2 Tim. 2:12).

For the accomplishing of the building up of the organic Body of Christ to fulfill the New Testament economy of God, we rule as kings over sin, the world, Satan, the natural man, the self, and individualism by the receiving of the abundance of grace through Christ...(Rom. 5:17). Grace is the divine life for our experience and enjoyment. The abundance of grace is just the abundance of the riches of the divine life.

The result of all the items by which we are saved in the divine life is the victory over Satan (16:20). Satan will be crushed under our feet. Satan is crushed, and we have God as our peace and Christ as our grace. We have such a life in which we enjoy the peace of God, which is God Himself, and the grace of the Lord, which is the Lord Himself. (*CWWL, 1990,* vol. 1, "The Triune God to Be Life to the Tripartite Man," pp. 289-290)

Our living with Christ is not aimless; it has a definite purpose. This purpose is to be one with Christ in His intercession for the churches, in His ministry of the heavenly life supply to the saints, and in His administration of God's government....The result of living together with the Lord in such a way is the new man. We cannot produce the new man by organization. The new man is the spontaneous issue of our taking Christ as our life and living Him.

The desire of God's heart is to have the new man. This was His plan in eternity past, and this was the reason He created the universe and accomplished redemption for us in Christ. The preaching of the gospel and the new creation are likewise for the new man. The time has come for God to have the new man expressed on earth. If we take Christ as our life and live together with Him, the new man will come forth to satisfy God's desire. (*Life-study of Colossians,* pp. 535-536)

Further Reading: CWWL, 1990, vol. 1, "The Triune God to Be Life to the Tripartite Man," chs. 6-7

Enlightenment and inspiration: _____

_____

_____

_____

Hymns, #505

1   There's a Man in the glory
    Whose Life is for me.
He's pure and He's holy,
    Triumphant and free.
He's wise and He's loving,
    How tender is He!
His Life in the glory,
    My life must be;
His Life in the glory,
    My life must be.

2   There's a Man in the glory
    Whose Life is for me.
He overcame Satan;
    From bondage He's free.
In Life He is reigning;
    How kingly is He!
His Life in the glory,
    My life must be;
His Life in the glory
    My life must be.

3   There's a Man in the glory
    Whose Life is for me.
In Him is no sickness;
    No weakness has He.
He's strong and in vigor,
    How buoyant is He!
His Life in the glory
    My life may be;
His Life in the glory
    My life may be.

4   There's a Man in the glory
    Whose Life is for me.
His peace is abiding;
    How patient is He!
He's joyful and radiant,
    Expecting to see
His Life in the glory
    Lived out in me;
His Life in the glory
    Lived out in me.

Composition for prophecy with main point and sub-points: _____

_____

_____

_____

_____

_____

_____

_____

_____

_____

_____

_____

_____

_____

_____

_____

_____

_____

_____

_____

_____

_____

_____

_____

_____

_____

_____

_____

_____

_____

_____

_____

_____

_____

***Allowing the Peace of Christ
to Arbitrate in Our Hearts,
Letting the Word of Christ
Dwell in Us Richly,
and Persevering in Prayer
for the One New Man***

Scripture Reading: Col. 3:15-17; 4:2-3

Day 1 I. **We need to allow the peace of Christ to arbitrate in our hearts (Col. 3:12-15; Eph. 2:14-18; Rom. 5:1; Matt. 18:21-35):**
   A. The Greek term for *arbitrate* can also be rendered "umpire, preside, or be enthroned as a ruler and decider of everything"; the arbitrating peace of Christ dissolves our complaint against anyone (Col. 3:13).
   B. Often we are conscious of three parties within us: a positive party, a negative party, and a neutral party; hence, there is the need for inward arbitration to settle the dispute within us:
      1. Whenever we sense that different parties within our being are arguing or quarreling, we need to give place to the presiding peace of Christ and allow this peace, which is the oneness of the new man, to rule within us and have the final word.
      2. We need to set aside our opinion, our concept, and listen to the word of the indwelling Referee.
Day 2   C. If we allow the peace of Christ to arbitrate in our hearts, this peace will settle all the disputes among us; we shall have peace with God vertically and with the saints horizontally:
      1. Through the arbitration of the peace of Christ, our problems are solved, and the friction between the saints disappears; then the church life is preserved in sweetness, and the new man is maintained in a practical way.

2. The arbitrating of the peace of Christ is Christ working within us to exercise His rule over us, to speak the last word, and to make the final decision (cf. Isa. 9:6-7).

3. If we stay under the ruling of the enthroned peace of Christ, we shall not offend others or damage them; rather, by the Lord's grace and with His peace we shall minister life to others.

4. This peace should bind all the believers together and become their uniting bond (Eph. 4:3).

Day 3　II. **We need to let the word of Christ dwell in us richly (Col. 3:16-17):**

A. When the peace of Christ arbitrates in us and keeps us in a situation full of oneness and harmony, we become the place of God's speaking, His oracle (vv. 15-16; Rev. 2:1, 7):

1. God's speaking requires oneness; division causes God's speaking to diminish, even to cease altogether (Lev. 1:1).

2. Since oneness is a necessary condition for God's speaking, we need to let the peace of Christ arbitrate in our hearts (Col. 3:15).

3. For the word of Christ to dwell in us richly means that it has adequate room in us to permeate and saturate our whole being; it is crucial for us to let the word of Christ enter into us, dwell in us, prevail in us, and replace our concepts, opinions, and philosophies (Psa. 119:130; cf. Rev. 21:23; 22:5).

Day 4　B. We need to allow the word of the Lord to have the first place in us so that we may experience the functions of the word of God operating within us and ministering the riches of Christ into our being (Col. 3:16):

1. The word of God enlightens (Psa. 119:105, 130), nourishes (Matt. 4:4; 1 Tim. 4:6), and waters us to quench our thirst (Isa. 55:8-11).

    2. The word of God strengthens (1 John 2:14b; Prov. 4:20-22), washes (Eph. 5:26), and builds us up (Acts 20:32).

    3. The word of God completes, perfects (2 Tim. 3:15-17), and edifies us by sanctifying us (John 17:17).

C. By allowing the word of God to inhabit us, we can become a proper human being, a God-man filled with Christ as the reality of the attributes of God (Col. 3:17-25; Phil. 4:5-8).

Day 5   **III. We need to persevere in prayer (Col. 4:2-3):**

A. We need to allow adequate time for prayer, which will enable us to absorb more of the riches of Christ as the all-inclusive land (1:12; 2:6-7; 4:2):

    1. We need to take time to absorb the Lord, contacting Him in a definite and prevailing way (Luke 8:13; Matt. 14:22-23; 6:6).

    2. To meet with God in the morning is not only to meet with Him early in the day; it is also to meet with God in a situation that is full of light; we should go to God alone, without any persons, matters, or things to distract or occupy us (Prov. 4:18; Exo. 33:11a; 34:3-4; Mark 1:35).

    3. When we pray, coming forward to the throne of grace, grace will become a river flowing in us and supplying us (Heb. 4:16; cf. Rev. 22:1).

B. In order to fight on God's side against Satan, we need to persevere in prayer (Dan. 6:10):

    1. As those who take sides with God, we find that the whole fallen universe is against us and, in particular, against our prayer; resistance to prayer lies not only outside of us but even within us (Matt. 26:41).

    2. To pray is to go against the current, the trend, in the fallen universe (Luke 18:1-8).

C. We need to set aside definite times for prayer; our attitude should be that prayer is our most important business and that nothing should be allowed to interfere with it (Dan. 6:10; Acts 12:5, 12).

Day 6   D. We need to remain in an atmosphere of prayer by continually exercising our spirit (Eph. 6:18; 1 Tim. 4:7; 2 Tim. 1:7; Col. 1:3, 9):

1. We need to pray without ceasing, to persevere in prayer, keeping ourselves intimately connected to the Lord (1 Thes. 5:17; Matt. 26:41; Col. 2:19).

2. Even in the smallest details we need to inquire of the Lord; to do this is to persevere in prayer and thereby to live Christ (cf. Josh. 9:14; Phil. 4:7-8).

IV. **As we are ruled by the peace of Christ and inhabited by the word of Christ through persevering in prayer, He permeates and replaces us with Himself until all our natural distinctions have been eliminated, and we become the new man in reality (Col. 3:15-17; 4:2-3; 3:10-11).**

Morning Nourishment

Col.   And let the peace of Christ arbitrate in your hearts,
3:15   to which also you were called in one Body; and be
       thankful.
Eph.   Abolishing in His flesh the law of the command-
2:15   ments in ordinances, that He might create the two
       in Himself into one new man, *so* making peace.

In Colossians 3:15...the Greek term for *arbitrate* can also be
rendered "umpire, preside, or be enthroned as a ruler and decider of everything." The arbitrating peace of Christ in our
hearts dissolves the complaint mentioned in verse 13.

The relative pronoun *which* in verse 15 refers to the peace of
Christ. We were called to this peace in the one Body of Christ.
For the proper Body life we need the peace of Christ to arbitrate, to adjust, to decide all things in our heart in the relationships between the members of His Body. Our having been
called to the peace of Christ should also motivate us to let this
peace arbitrate in our hearts. (*Life-study of Colossians*, p. 242)

Today's Reading

If we consider our experience, we shall realize that as Christians we have two or three parties within us....Often we are conscious of three parties within us: a positive party, a negative
party, and a neutral party. As Christians, we are more compli-
cated than unsaved people are. Before we were saved, we were
under the control of the satanic party. We could indulge in
worldly amusements and entertainments without any sense of
controversy within. But now that we are saved, one party may
encourage us to do one thing, but another party may encourage
us to do something else. Hence, there is the need for inward arbitration to settle the dispute within us. We need someone or
something to preside over the conferences that take place within
our being. According to Colossians 3:15, this presiding one, this
arbitrator, is the peace of Christ.

After Paul wrote concerning the all-inclusive Christ and concerning the new man in whom Christ is all and in all and where

there is no room for Greek, Jew, or other cultural distinctions, he charged the saints to care for the peace of Christ. Within us we all have something called the peace of Christ. This is the peace about which Paul speaks in Ephesians 2:15, where we are told that in Himself Christ created one new man out of two peoples. By creating the Jews and the Gentiles into one new man, Christ has made peace. This is the very peace in Colossians 3:15.

Believers with different cultural backgrounds and nationalities have been created into one new man. The oneness of the new man produces genuine peace. Apart from Christ and the church, those of different races and nationalities cannot be truly one....In the new man there are no different races, classes, or nationalities. Rather, there is oneness because Christ is all and in all. This oneness is our peace. The peace of Christ in Colossians 3:15 is simply the peaceful oneness in the new man.

We should allow the peace of Christ to arbitrate in our hearts. All the parties must take heed to the word of the arbitrator.... Whenever we sense that different parties within our being are arguing or quarreling, we need to give place to the presiding peace of Christ and allow this peace, which is the oneness of the new man, to rule within us. Let this peace, this oneness, have the final word.

The peace of Christ is the very oneness of the new man composed of different peoples. Apart from the work of Christ on the cross, there can be no oneness among the different peoples. But through His death Christ has made peace; that is, He has produced oneness. This oneness of the new man is now within us. This oneness, the peace of Christ, must now be permitted to arbitrate in our hearts. It should function as a referee to settle the disputes among various parties. We need to set aside our opinion, our concept, and listen to the word of the indwelling referee. There is no need for us to quarrel or to express our opinion. We should simply let the peace of Christ make the final decision. (*Life-study of Colossians,* pp. 242-245, 265)

Further Reading: Life-study of Colossians, msgs. 28-29, 32

Enlightenment and inspiration: _____

_____
_____
_____

Morning Nourishment

Col. **And let the peace of Christ arbitrate in your hearts,**
3:15 **to which also you were called in one Body...**
Eph. **Being diligent to keep the oneness of the Spirit in**
4:3 **the uniting bond of peace.**

In Colossians 3:15 and 16 Paul charges us to let the peace of Christ arbitrate in our hearts and to let the word of Christ dwell in us richly. If we allow the peace of Christ to arbitrate in our hearts, this peace will settle all the disputes among us. The saints in Colossae were troubled by different isms, philosophies, and practices....The Colossians needed a referee, an arbitrator, to calm down all the differing opinions,...which have their source in...culture. (*Life-study of Colossians*, pp. 276-277)

Today's Reading

For the peace of Christ to arbitrate in our hearts, it must rule in us. It must be enthroned as the ruler and decider....Let us take as an example a brother who is offended by one of the elders....In His mercy, the Lord will come to him and cause him to set his mind on the things above so that once again he can experience the divine transmission which gives rise to the arbitrating peace of Christ. Then, ruled by the peace of Christ, the brother will admit that even though the elder might have been wrong, he himself was wrong to a greater degree. Immediately he will confess to the Lord, receive grace, and have love for that elder. Through the arbitration of the peace of Christ, our problems are solved, and the friction between the saints disappears. Then the church life is preserved, and the new man is maintained in a practical way.

The church life as the life of the new man is preserved not by mere teachings but by setting our mind on the things above and allowing the heavenly transmission to impart the divine element into us. Then we shall have the renewing of the new man and experience the peace of Christ ruling within us. The peace of Christ is actually Christ Himself in a particular aspect. Hence, the arbitrating of the peace of Christ is Christ working within us to exercise His rule over us, to speak the last word, and to make the final decision. In the case of the brother offended by the elder, Christ's word is to love that elder, to seek him out for fellowship, and to enjoy the Lord with him. This is Christ enthroned as peace ruling, deciding, and uttering the last word.

When the peace of Christ is enthroned in our hearts to be the unique umpire within us, we shall have peace with God vertically and with the saints horizontally. We praise the Lord that we are enjoying peace, and in this peace the church life as the new man is preserved! As the peace of Christ presides in our hearts, the renewing of the new man takes place continually. If we stay under the ruling of the enthroned peace of Christ, we shall not offend others or damage them. Rather, by the Lord's grace and with His peace, we shall minister life to others. The oneness in a local church and among the churches is not maintained by human endeavoring. It is maintained only by the arbitrating peace of Christ....All the churches and the recovery as a whole are under the arbitrating peace of Christ. In us Christ is the supplying grace and the arbitrating peace....If we allow the enthroned peace of Christ to arbitrate in our hearts, our married life, family life, and church life will all be preserved in oneness.

May we be encouraged to set our mind on the things above so that the heavenly transmission may bring the divine substance into our being for the renewing of the new man. Then Christ in the particular aspect of peace will arbitrate in our hearts, and the Lord will have a way to build up the new man and prepare the bride for His coming. (*Life-study of Colossians,* pp. 564-566)

Christ abolished on the cross all the differences that were due to ordinances. In so doing He made peace for His Body. This peace should bind all believers together and should thus become the uniting bond. The uniting bond of peace is the issue of the working of the cross. When we remain on the cross, we have peace with others. This peace becomes the uniting bond in which we keep the oneness of the Spirit. (Eph. 4:3, footnote 3)

Further Reading: Life-study of Colossians, msgs. 33, 63

Enlightenment and inspiration: _____

_____

_____

_____

Morning Nourishment

Col. And let the peace of Christ arbitrate in your hearts....
3:15-16 Let the word of Christ dwell in you richly...
Psa. The opening of Your words gives light, imparting
119:130 understanding to the simple.
Rev. He who has an ear, let him hear what the Spirit
2:7 says to the churches...

Immediately after speaking about the peace of Christ arbitrating in us [in Colossians 3:15], Paul goes on to tell us to let the word of Christ dwell in us [v. 16]. Why does Paul mention the peace of Christ before the word of Christ? The answer to this question is related to the basic principle revealed in the Bible that God's speaking requires oneness. Whenever God's people are divided, His word becomes rare. God does not speak where there is division. Division causes God's speaking to diminish, even to cease altogether.

When the children of Israel were in the wilderness, God spoke in the Tent of Meeting. The Tent of Meeting was a sign of the oneness of God's people. The twelve tribes were arranged around the Tent of Meeting, and God spoke to the people from within the Tent of Meeting. Any Israelite at that time who wanted God's speaking had to come to the Tent of Meeting, the place of oneness....The temple built in Jerusalem was the continuation of the Tent of Meeting....God's speaking through the priests came out of the Holy of Holies, the center both of the tabernacle and of the temple. (*Life-study of Colossians,* pp. 567-568)

Today's Reading

If we are truly one with other members of the Body of Christ, we shall be able to speak God's word. However, if we are not one with the saints but are filled with murmuring, complaining, and gossiping about others, we shall not be able to speak the word of the Lord. Speaking God's word requires oneness. Where there is no oneness, there can be no speaking. If we allow the peace of Christ to arbitrate in us to maintain oneness and harmony, we shall be able to speak the word of God.

When the peace of Christ arbitrates in us and keeps us in a

situation full of oneness and harmony, we become the place of God's speaking, His oracle.

The word of Christ is the word spoken by Christ. In His New Testament economy God speaks in the Son, and the Son speaks not only directly in the Gospels, but also through His members, the apostles and prophets, in Acts, in the Epistles, and in Revelation. All these may be considered as His word.

The word of Christ includes the entire New Testament. We need to be filled with this word. This means that we should allow the word of Christ to dwell in us, to inhabit us, to make home in us. [In Colossians 3:16] the Greek word rendered "dwell" means "to be in a house, to inhabit." The word of the Lord must have adequate room within us so that it may operate and minister the riches of Christ into our inner being. Furthermore, the word of Christ must dwell in us richly. The riches of Christ (Eph. 3:8) are in His word. When such a rich word inhabits us, it must inhabit us richly. The word of Christ should have [a] free course...to operate within us.

Certain saints love the Bible and read it daily....Although they read the Bible, God's word remains outside of them. It is crucial for us to let the word of Christ enter into us, dwell in us, and replace our concepts, opinions, and philosophies. We need to pray, "Lord Jesus, I am willing to let go of my concepts. I want Your word to have ground in me. I am willing to forget my opinion and philosophy. I want Your word to be prevailing in me. I do not want my concepts to prevail any longer."

We cannot separate the word of Christ from His arbitration. The arbitrator settles a dispute by speaking a word. We need to bring our case to the arbitrator and listen to his word. This means that we need to allow the peace of Christ to arbitrate in our hearts and the word of Christ to dwell in us. Then we shall be filled with singing and giving of thanks. (*Life-study of Colossians,* pp. 569-570, 245-247)

Further Reading: Life-study of Colossians, msgs. 47, 52, 58

Enlightenment and inspiration: _____

_____

_____

_____

Morning Nourishment

Lev. Then Jehovah called to Moses and spoke to him out
1:1 of the Tent of Meeting...
Col. Let the word of Christ dwell in you richly in all
3:16-17 wisdom, teaching and admonishing one another with
psalms *and* hymns *and* spiritual songs, singing with
grace in your hearts to God. And whatever you do in
word or in deed, *do all things in the name of the Lord
Jesus, giving thanks to God the Father through Him.*

If the word of Christ is to make its home in us, we must give
it the full liberty, freedom, and right. We need to pray, "Lord,
I offer my whole being to You and Your word. I give You access
to every part of my inner being. Lord, make my inner being a
home for Yourself and Your word."

Outwardly we may act as if the first place is reserved for the
word of God. But secretly the first place is for us.

Suppose you are reading Matthew 19:16-22, where the Lord
Jesus tells the young man to sell all that he has, give to the poor,
and follow Him. As you read this portion of Scripture, the Lord may
tell you to give away certain things. That would be a test of what is
first—the self or the word of God. Many of us have learned from
experience how difficult it is for us to give first place to the word of
God. For this, we need the Lord's grace. We need to turn to the
Lord and say, "Lord, I cannot do this, but, Lord, You can. Lord, I
trust in You for this." (*Life-study of Colossians,* pp. 574-575)

Today's Reading

We need the arbitrating peace of Christ to preserve us in oneness that the Lord may speak to us. Then we need to give first place
to the word of God. If we do this, we shall experience the functions
of the word of God: enlightening, nourishing, quenching our thirst,
strengthening, washing, building, perfecting, and edifying.

First, the word of God enlightens us. If we did not have the
Word, we would be in darkness. But because God's word is full of
light and it enlightens us, it can make us very clear about many
different things.

Second, the word of God is food, full of nourishment. This means that God's word nourishes us while it enlightens us. I can testify that throughout the years I have been adequately nourished through the word of God.

The word of God also quenches our thirst....Usually a person can go longer without eating than without drinking. If we do not have water, we simply have no way to live. How good that the word of God is not only food, but also the water of life! The word of God enlightens us, feeds us, and quenches our thirst.

The word of God makes us strong in spirit and also in soul. Strengthened in spirit and soul, we shall be healthy in body. The word of God is the best cure; it strengthens us and it heals us.

The word of God also washes us. It washes our being organically and metabolically. When God's word enters into our fibers organically, it washes us metabolically.

Furthermore, the word of God builds us up. As members of the church, the Body, we all need to be built up. Because we are peculiar, it is difficult for anyone to deal with us, much less to build us together. However, the word of God can touch us inwardly and make it possible for us to be built up in the church.

The word of God also completes and perfects....As members of the Body, we all should function. But if we would function, we first need to be perfected by the word of God. Because God's word nourishes us, we have growth. Then through the growth, the functions come forth. The nourishment we receive from the word of God completes us and perfects us as members of the Body.

The last function of the word of God...is its function of edifying us....Being built up is related to the church corporately. Being edified involves being built up individually, primarily in the matter of virtues. We all need to be edified, or built up in a personal way, for we all lack certain virtues....Our kindness, patience, wisdom, and humility will all be increased by the word of God. (*Life-study of Colossians,* pp. 575, 571-573)

Further Reading: Life-study of Colossians, msg. 64

Enlightenment and inspiration: _____

_____

_____

_____

Morning Nourishment

Col. **As therefore you have received the Christ, Jesus the**
2:6-7 **Lord, walk in Him, having been rooted and being**
       built up in Him, and being established in the faith
       even as you were taught, abounding in thanksgiving.
  4:2 **Persevere in prayer, watching in it with thanksgiving.**

Our need is to take time to absorb God. As we daily take time
to eat food, we should daily take time to absorb the Lord, take
time to assimilate the riches of Christ. Our contact with the Lord
should not be rushed. If we are in a hurry, we shall not be able to
absorb much of His riches. We need to allow adequate time for
prayer. This will enable us to absorb more of the riches of our
God. (*Life-study of Colossians*, p. 456)

Since our need today is to be filled and saturated with the
Spirit, we must consider what we need to do in order to experience
the Spirit. The Lord's Word reveals that on God's side everything is
ready. God is ready and is waiting for us....The first thing we must
do is to go to the Lord. To do this we need to learn how to contact the
Lord in a definite and prevailing way. I am afraid that many believers have been praying for a number of years and have spent much
time reading the Word but have never contacted the Lord in a definite and prevailing way. (*Contacting the Lord, Being Filled in
Spirit, and Having Proper Christian Meetings for the Accomplishment of God's Eternal Purpose*, p. 35)

Today's Reading

To persevere in prayer is to continue persistently, steadfastly,
and earnestly....We need to persevere in prayer because prayer involves a battle, a fight. Two parties, God and Satan, are hostile to
each other. The meaning of the name Satan is adversary. Satan is
both the enemy without and the adversary within....As the adversary, Satan opposes God from within God's realm, God's kingdom.

Although the battle raging in the universe is between God and
Satan,...it is necessary for another of God's creatures—man—to
fight against Satan. In a very real sense, God needs us. Without
us, He would not have a way to carry on the battle against

Satan....He needs us to carry on the actual work of warfare.

In order to fight on God's side against Satan, we need to persevere in prayer. This perseverance is needed because the course of the whole world is away from God. To pray is to go against the current, the trend, in the fallen universe. Persevering in prayer is like rowing a boat upstream. If you do not persevere, you will be carried downstream by the current....As those who take sides with God, we find that the whole universe is against us and, in particular, against our prayer.

In light of the fact that there is great resistance to praying, let us now consider in a very practical way how to persevere in prayer. Before you try to persevere in prayer, you should first make a deal with the Lord concerning your prayer life....We need to say to Him, "Lord, I am desperate about this. I offer myself to You so that I may have a prayer life. Lord, keep me in the spirit of prayer. If I forget this or neglect this, I know that You will not forget it. Remind me again and again about prayer."

After we make such a deal with the Lord concerning prayer, we should set aside definite times for prayer. For instance, you may reserve ten minutes every morning. During this time, prayer must be the top priority. Our attitude should be that prayer is our most important business and that nothing should be allowed to interfere with it. If we do not have this attitude, we shall not be able to have a successful prayer life. No matter how many things we have to do each day, we can reserve at least a few minutes here and there for prayer. We may pray a little in the morning. Then again at noon, after work, and in the evening we may have other times for prayer. By setting aside definite times during the day, we may be able to have a half hour reserved for prayer. (*Life-study of Colossians*, pp. 577-580)

Further Reading: Life-study of Colossians, msgs. 30, 53, 55; *Contacting the Lord, Being Filled in Spirit, and Having Proper Christian Meetings for the Accomplishment of God's Eternal Purpose,* ch. 3

Enlightenment and inspiration: _____

_____

_____

_____

Morning Nourishment

1 Tim. I exhort therefore, first of all, that petitions, prayers,
2:1 intercessions, thanksgivings be made on behalf of
all men.

Col. We give thanks to God, the Father of our Lord Jesus
1:3 Christ, praying always concerning you.

9 Therefore we also, since the day we heard of *it*, do
not cease praying and asking on your behalf...

1 Thes. Unceasingly pray.
5:17

To have uninterrupted fellowship with God in our spirit... requires perseverance (Rom. 12:12; Col. 4:2) with a strong spirit (Eph. 6:18). (1 Thes. 5:17, footnote 1)

When you are observing a set time for prayer at home, take the telephone off the hook...[and do] not pay attention to those knocking at your door. The time you have dedicated to the Lord for prayer should be used only for prayer, not for anything else. Regarding this, you need to be strong and persevering.

As far as prayer is concerned,...I have suffered many failures because of the opposition of the enemy, the distractions around me, and even the hindrances within me....Because [prayer] is a battle, a fight, we must persevere in it.

When we pray, we enter into the Holy of Holies and approach the throne of grace....When we pray, approaching the throne of grace, mercy and grace will become a river flowing in us and supplying us. How rewarding this is! Receiving the flow of grace in prayer is actually more important than having our prayers answered. (*Life-study of Colossians*, pp. 580-582)

Today's Reading

If we would experience Christ and live Him, we need to remain in an atmosphere of prayer. Many of us can testify that by prayer we are brought into the spirit, where we are one with the Lord and take Him as our life. This experience is so precious that when we are enjoying it, we do not want it to end....However, as soon as our time of prayer is over, most of the time we revert to our natural way of living. We are no longer in an atmosphere of prayer. Automatically we begin to try once again to be holy, spiritual, and victorious. Whenever we fail, we repent, confess to the Lord, and resolve to try again. This is not the way to live the Christian life. On the contrary, our daily living should be the same as our experience in genuine prayer....To live Christ it is necessary to persevere in prayer, to pray without ceasing. We need to stay in the atmosphere of prayer.

Our need is to contact this living person in prayer. Then we need to remain in an atmosphere of prayer. If we do this, we shall live Christ spontaneously. Furthermore, we shall be freed from our culture without trying to adjust or correct ourselves. Everything other than Christ will fade away. Christ will be whatever we need: life, light, grace, comfort, health, strength, humility, patience, kindness, meekness.

As we enjoy the Lord and experience Him, He will be our life and we shall live Him. How marvelous! This is what Paul means in Philippians 1:21: "For to me, to live is Christ."

In order to live Christ, we need to pray without ceasing. As soon as we stop praying, we stop living Christ.

Persevering in prayer has many benefits. By prayer we set our mind on the things above....When we set our mind on the things above during our times of prayer, we become a reflection of Christ's ministry in the heavens. Through our prayer, Christ, the Head, is given a way to carry out His administration through His Body.

It is always difficult at first to have a proper prayer life. But if you practice this for a long period of time, it will get easier and easier, for you will realize the rewards of praying.

We have seen that for a normal Christian walk we need to set our mind on things above, have the renewing of the new man, have the peace of Christ arbitrating in us, and allow the word of Christ to inhabit us. These four matters, however, all require prayer. To practice them and to experience them we need to pray. Prayer ushers us into the reality of these four things and keeps us in this reality. (*Life-study of Colossians*, pp. 334-336, 581-583)

Further Reading: Life-study of Colossians, msgs. 35, 39, 65

Enlightenment and inspiration: _____

_____

_____

_____

Hymns, #189

1   Thou art the Son beloved,
      The image of our God;
    Thou art the saints' dear portion,
      Imparted thru Thy blood.
    Among all God's creation
      Thou art the firstborn One;
    By Thee all was created,
      All for Thyself to own.

2   Thou art before all creatures,
      In Thee all things consist;
    Of all Thou art the center,
      By Thee all things subsist.
    Thou art the sole beginning,
      The Firstborn from the dead;
    And for the church, Thy Body,
      Thou art the glorious Head.

3   Because it pleased the Father,
      All fulness dwells in Thee,
    That Thou might have the first place
      In all we ever see.
    All things Thou reconciledst
      To God by Thy shed blood,
    To thus present us holy
      And blameless unto God.

4   In Thee God's fulness dwelleth,
      Thou art God's mystery;
    The treasures of all wisdom
      And knowledge are in Thee.
    Thou art the hope of glory,
      In us Thou dost abide;
    In Thee we are perfected
      And God is satisfied.

5   All things are but a shadow
      Which unto us reveal
    Thyself, in whom we're rooted,
      The only One that's real.
    Enjoying all Thy riches,
      Thy fulness we will be;
    We'll hold Thee, as Thy Body,
      And grow with God in Thee.

6 With Thee in God we're hidden,
      Thou art in us our life;
   Thy peace in us presiding,
      We rest from all our strife.
   In the new man, Thy Body,
      Thou art the all in all;
   Our all-inclusive Savior,
      Thyself we'll ever call.

Composition for prophecy with main point and sub-points: _____

_____

_____

_____

_____

_____

_____

_____

_____

_____

_____

_____

_____

_____

_____

_____

_____

_____

_____

_____

_____

_____

_____

_____

_____

_____

Reading Schedule for the Recovery Version of the Old Testament with Footnotes

Wk.	Lord's Day	Monday	Tuesday	Wednesday	Thursday	Friday	Saturday
1	Gen. 1:1-5 ☐	1:6-23 ☐	1:24-31 ☐	2:1-9 ☐	2:10-25 ☐	3:1-13 ☐	3:14-24 ☐
2	4:1-26 ☐	5:1-32 ☐	6:1-22 ☐	7:1—8:3 ☐	8:4-22 ☐	9:1-29 ☐	10:1-32 ☐
3	11:1-32 ☐	12:1-20 ☐	13:1-18 ☐	14:1-24 ☐	15:1-21 ☐	16:1-16 ☐	17:1-27 ☐
4	18:1-33 ☐	19:1-38 ☐	20:1-18 ☐	21:1-34 ☐	22:1-24 ☐	23:1—24:27 ☐	24:28-67 ☐
5	25:1-34 ☐	26:1-35 ☐	27:1-46 ☐	28:1-22 ☐	29:1-35 ☐	30:1-43 ☐	31:1-55 ☐
6	32:1-32 ☐	33:1—34:31 ☐	35:1-29 ☐	36:1-43 ☐	37:1-36 ☐	38:1—39:23 ☐	40:1—41:13 ☐
7	41:14-57 ☐	42:1-38 ☐	43:1-34 ☐	44:1-34 ☐	45:1-28 ☐	46:1-34 ☐	47:1-31 ☐
8	48:1-22 ☐	49:1-15 ☐	49:16-33 ☐	50:1-26 ☐	Exo. 1:1-22 ☐	2:1-25 ☐	3:1-22 ☐
9	4:1-31 ☐	5:1-23 ☐	6:1-30 ☐	7:1-25 ☐	8:1-32 ☐	9:1-35 ☐	10:1-29 ☐
10	11:1-10 ☐	12:1-14 ☐	12:15-36 ☐	12:37-51 ☐	13:1-22 ☐	14:1-31 ☐	15:1-27 ☐
11	16:1-36 ☐	17:1-16 ☐	18:1-27 ☐	19:1-25 ☐	20:1-26 ☐	21:1-36 ☐	22:1-31 ☐
12	23:1-33 ☐	24:1-18 ☐	25:1-22 ☐	25:23-40 ☐	26:1-14 ☐	26:15-37 ☐	27:1-21 ☐
13	28:1-21 ☐	28:22-43 ☐	29:1-21 ☐	29:22-46 ☐	30:1-10 ☐	30:11-38 ☐	31:1-17 ☐
14	31:18—32:35 ☐	33:1-23 ☐	34:1-35 ☐	35:1-35 ☐	36:1-38 ☐	37:1-29 ☐	38:1-31 ☐
15	39:1-43 ☐	40:1-38 ☐	Lev. 1:1-17 ☐	2:1-16 ☐	3:1-17 ☐	4:1-35 ☐	5:1-19 ☐
16	6:1-30 ☐	7:1-38 ☐	8:1-36 ☐	9:1-24 ☐	10:1-20 ☐	11:1-47 ☐	12:1-8 ☐
17	13:1-28 ☐	13:29-59 ☐	14:1-18 ☐	14:19-32 ☐	14:33-57 ☐	15:1-33 ☐	16:1-17 ☐
18	16:18-34 ☐	17:1-16 ☐	18:1-30 ☐	19:1-37 ☐	20:1-27 ☐	21:1-24 ☐	22:1-33 ☐
19	23:1-22 ☐	23:23-44 ☐	24:1-23 ☐	25:1-23 ☐	25:24-55 ☐	26:1-24 ☐	26:25-46 ☐
20	27:1-34 ☐	Num. 1:1-54 ☐	2:1-34 ☐	3:1-51 ☐	4:1-49 ☐	5:1-31 ☐	6:1-27 ☐
21	7:1-41 ☐	7:42-88 ☐	7:89—8:26 ☐	9:1-23 ☐	10:1-36 ☐	11:1-35 ☐	12:1—13:33 ☐
22	14:1-45 ☐	15:1-41 ☐	16:1-50 ☐	17:1—18:7 ☐	18:8-32 ☐	19:1-22 ☐	20:1-29 ☐
23	21:1-35 ☐	22:1-41 ☐	23:1-30 ☐	24:1-25 ☐	25:1-18 ☐	26:1-65 ☐	27:1-23 ☐
24	28:1-31 ☐	29:1-40 ☐	30:1—31:24 ☐	31:25-54 ☐	32:1-42 ☐	33:1-56 ☐	34:1-29 ☐
25	35:1-34 ☐	36:1-13 ☐	Deut. 1:1-46 ☐	2:1-37 ☐	3:1-29 ☐	4:1-49 ☐	5:1-33 ☐
26	6:1—7:26 ☐	8:1-20 ☐	9:1-29 ☐	10:1-22 ☐	11:1-32 ☐	12:1-32 ☐	13:1—14:21 ☐

Reading Schedule for the Recovery Version of the Old Testament with Footnotes

Wk.	Lord's Day	Monday	Tuesday	Wednesday	Thursday	Friday	Saturday
27	☐ 14:22—15:23	☐ 16:1-22	☐ 17:1—18:8	☐ 18:9—19:21	☐ 20:1—21:17	☐ 21:18—22:30	☐ 23:1-25
28	☐ 24:1-22	☐ 25:1-19	☐ 26:1-19	☐ 27:1-26	☐ 28:1-68	☐ 29:1-29	☐ 30:1—31:29
29	☐ 31:30—32:52	☐ 33:1-29	☐ 34:1-12	☐ Josh. 1:1-18	☐ 2:1-24	☐ 3:1-17	☐ 4:1-24
30	☐ 5:1-15	☐ 6:1-27	☐ 7:1-26	☐ 8:1-35	☐ 9:1-27	☐ 10:1-43	☐ 11:1—12:24
31	☐ 13:1-33	☐ 14:1—15:63	☐ 16:1—18:28	☐ 19:1-51	☐ 20:1—21:45	☐ 22:1-34	☐ 23:1—24:33
32	☐ Judg. 1:1-36	☐ 2:1-23	☐ 3:1-31	☐ 4:1-24	☐ 5:1-31	☐ 6:1-40	☐ 7:1-25
33	☐ 8:1-35	☐ 9:1-57	☐ 10:1—11:40	☐ 12:1—13:25	☐ 14:1—15:20	☐ 16:1-31	☐ 17:1—18:31
34	☐ 19:1-30	☐ 20:1-48	☐ 21:1-25	☐ Ruth 1:1-22	☐ 2:1-23	☐ 3:1-18	☐ 4:1-22
35	☐ 1 Sam. 1:1-28	☐ 2:1-36	☐ 3:1—4:22	☐ 5:1—6:21	☐ 7:1—8:22	☐ 9:1-27	☐ 10:1—11:15
36	☐ 12:1—13:23	☐ 14:1-52	☐ 15:1-35	☐ 16:1-23	☐ 17:1-58	☐ 18:1-30	☐ 19:1-24
37	☐ 20:1-42	☐ 21:1—22:23	☐ 23:1—24:22	☐ 25:1-44	☐ 26:1-25	☐ 27:1—28:25	☐ 29:1—30:31
38	☐ 31:1-13	☐ 2 Sam. 1:1-27	☐ 2:1-32	☐ 3:1-39	☐ 4:1—5:25	☐ 6:1-23	☐ 7:1-29
39	☐ 8:1—9:13	☐ 10:1—11:27	☐ 12:1-31	☐ 13:1-39	☐ 14:1-33	☐ 15:1—16:23	☐ 17:1—18:33
40	☐ 19:1-43	☐ 20:1—21:22	☐ 22:1-51	☐ 23:1-39	☐ 24:1-25	☐ 1 Kings 1:1-19	☐ 1:20-53
41	☐ 2:1-46	☐ 3:1-28	☐ 4:1-34	☐ 5:1—6:38	☐ 7:1-22	☐ 7:23-51	☐ 8:1-36
42	☐ 8:37-66	☐ 9:1-28	☐ 10:1-29	☐ 11:1-43	☐ 12:1-33	☐ 13:1-34	☐ 14:1-31
43	☐ 15:1-34	☐ 16:1—17:24	☐ 18:1-46	☐ 19:1-21	☐ 20:1-43	☐ 21:1—22:53	☐ 2 Kings 1:1-18
44	☐ 2:1—3:27	☐ 4:1-44	☐ 5:1—6:33	☐ 7:1-20	☐ 8:1-29	☐ 9:1-37	☐ 10:1-36
45	☐ 11:1—12:21	☐ 13:1—14:29	☐ 15:1-38	☐ 16:1-20	☐ 17:1-41	☐ 18:1-37	☐ 19:1-37
46	☐ 20:1—21:26	☐ 22:1-20	☐ 23:1-37	☐ 24:1—25:30	☐ 1 Chron. 1:1-54	☐ 2:1—3:24	☐ 4:1—5:26
47	☐ 6:1-81	☐ 7:1-40	☐ 8:1-40	☐ 9:1-44	☐ 10:1—11:47	☐ 12:1-40	☐ 13:1—14:17
48	☐ 15:1—16:43	☐ 17:1-27	☐ 18:1—19:19	☐ 20:1—21:30	☐ 22:1—23:32	☐ 24:1—25:31	☐ 26:1-32
49	☐ 27:1-34	☐ 28:1—29:30	☐ 2 Chron. 1:1-17	☐ 2:1—3:17	☐ 4:1—5:14	☐ 6:1-42	☐ 7:1—8:18
50	☐ 9:1—10:19	☐ 11:1—12:16	☐ 13:1—15:19	☐ 16:1—17:19	☐ 18:1—19:11	☐ 20:1-37	☐ 21:1—22:12
51	☐ 23:1—24:27	☐ 25:1—26:23	☐ 27:1—28:27	☐ 29:1-36	☐ 30:1—31:21	☐ 32:1-33	☐ 33:1—34:33
52	☐ 35:1—36:23	☐ Ezra 1:1-11	☐ 2:1-70	☐ 3:1—4:24	☐ 5:1—6:22	☐ 7:1-28	☐ 8:1-36

Reading Schedule for the Recovery Version of the Old Testament with Footnotes

Wk.	Lord's Day	Monday	Tuesday	Wednesday	Thursday	Friday	Saturday
53	9:1—10:44 ☐	Neh. 1:1-11 ☐	2:1—3:32 ☐	4:1—5:19 ☐	6:1-19 ☐	7:1-73 ☐	8:1-18 ☐
54	9:1-20 ☐	9:21-38 ☐	10:1—11:36 ☐	12:1-47 ☐	13:1-31 ☐	Esth. 1:1-22 ☐	2:1—3:15 ☐
55	4:1—5:14 ☐	6:1—7:10 ☐	8:1-17 ☐	9:1—10:3 ☐	Job 1:1-22 ☐	2:1—3:26 ☐	4:1—5:27 ☐
56	6:1—7:21 ☐	8:1—9:35 ☐	10:1—11:20 ☐	12:1—13:28 ☐	14:1—15:35 ☐	16:1—17:16 ☐	18:1—19:29 ☐
57	20:1—21:34 ☐	22:1—23:17 ☐	24:1—25:6 ☐	26:1—27:23 ☐	28:1—29:25 ☐	30:1—31:40 ☐	32:1—33:33 ☐
58	34:1—35:16 ☐	36:1-33 ☐	37:1-24 ☐	38:1-41 ☐	39:1-30 ☐	40:1-24 ☐	41:1-34 ☐
59	42:1-17 ☐	Psa. 1:1-6 ☐	2:1—3:8 ☐	4:1—6:10 ☐	7:1—8:9 ☐	9:1—10:18 ☐	11:1—15:5 ☐
60	16:1—17:15 ☐	18:1-50 ☐	19:1—21:13 ☐	22:1-31 ☐	23:1—24:10 ☐	25:1—27:14 ☐	28:1—30:12 ☐
61	31:1—32:11 ☐	33:1—34:22 ☐	35:1—36:12 ☐	37:1-40 ☐	38:1—39:13 ☐	40:1—41:13 ☐	42:1—43:5 ☐
62	44:1-26 ☐	45:1-17 ☐	46:1—48:14 ☐	49:1—50:23 ☐	51:1—52:9 ☐	53:1—55:23 ☐	56:1—58:11 ☐
63	59:1—61:8 ☐	62:1—64:10 ☐	65:1—67:7 ☐	68:1-35 ☐	69:1—70:5 ☐	71:1—72:20 ☐	73:1—74:23 ☐
64	75:1—77:20 ☐	78:1-72 ☐	79:1—81:16 ☐	82:1—84:12 ☐	85:1—87:7 ☐	88:1—89:52 ☐	90:1—91:16 ☐
65	92:1—94:23 ☐	95:1—97:12 ☐	98:1—101:8 ☐	102:1—103:22 ☐	104:1—105:45 ☐	106:1-48 ☐	107:1-43 ☐
66	108:1—109:31 ☐	110:1—112:10 ☐	113:1—115:18 ☐	116:1—118:29 ☐	119:1-32 ☐	119:33-72 ☐	119:73-120 ☐
67	119:121-176 ☐	120:1—124:8 ☐	125:1—128:6 ☐	129:1—132:18 ☐	133:1—135:21 ☐	136:1—138:8 ☐	139:1—140:13 ☐
68	141:1—144:15 ☐	145:1—147:20 ☐	148:1—150:6 ☐	Prov. 1:1-33 ☐	2:1—3:35 ☐	4:1—5:23 ☐	6:1-35 ☐
69	7:1—8:36 ☐	9:1—10:32 ☐	11:1—12:28 ☐	13:1—14:35 ☐	15:1-33 ☐	16:1-33 ☐	17:1-28 ☐
70	18:1-24 ☐	19:1—20:30 ☐	21:1—22:29 ☐	23:1-35 ☐	24:1—25:28 ☐	26:1—27:27 ☐	28:1—29:27 ☐
71	30:1-33 ☐	31:1-31 ☐	Eccl. 1:1-18 ☐	2:1—3:22 ☐	4:1—5:20 ☐	6:1—7:29 ☐	8:1—9:18 ☐
72	10:1—11:10 ☐	12:1-14 ☐	S.S. 1:1-8 ☐	1:9-17 ☐	2:1-17 ☐	3:1-11 ☐	4:1-8 ☐
73	4:9-16 ☐	5:1-16 ☐	6:1-13 ☐	7:1-13 ☐	8:1-14 ☐	Isa. 1:1-11 ☐	1:12-31 ☐
74	2:1-22 ☐	3:1-26 ☐	4:1-6 ☐	5:1-30 ☐	6:1-13 ☐	7:1-25 ☐	8:1-22 ☐
75	9:1-21 ☐	10:1-34 ☐	11:1—12:6 ☐	13:1-22 ☐	14:1-14 ☐	14:15-32 ☐	15:1—16:14 ☐
76	17:1—18:7 ☐	19:1-25 ☐	20:1—21:17 ☐	22:1-25 ☐	23:1-18 ☐	24:1-23 ☐	25:1-12 ☐
77	26:1-21 ☐	27:1-13 ☐	28:1-29 ☐	29:1-24 ☐	30:1-33 ☐	31:1—32:20 ☐	33:1-24 ☐
78	34:1-17 ☐	35:1-10 ☐	36:1-22 ☐	37:1-38 ☐	38:1—39:8 ☐	40:1-31 ☐	41:1-29 ☐

Reading Schedule for the Recovery Version of the Old Testament with Footnotes

Wk.	Lord's Day	Monday	Tuesday	Wednesday	Thursday	Friday	Saturday
79	42:1-25 ☐	43:1-28 ☐	44:1-28 ☐	45:1-25 ☐	46:1-13 ☐	47:1-15 ☐	48:1-22 ☐
80	49:1-13 ☐	49:14-26 ☐	50:1—51:23 ☐	52:1-15 ☐	53:1-12 ☐	54:1-17 ☐	55:1-13 ☐
81	56:1-12 ☐	57:1-21 ☐	58:1-14 ☐	59:1-21 ☐	60:1-22 ☐	61:1-11 ☐	62:1-12 ☐
82	63:1-19 ☐	64:1-12 ☐	65:1-25 ☐	66:1-24 ☐	Jer. 1:1-19 ☐	2:1-19 ☐	2:20-37 ☐
83	3:1-25 ☐	4:1-31 ☐	5:1-31 ☐	6:1-30 ☐	7:1-34 ☐	8:1-22 ☐	9:1-26 ☐
84	10:1-25 ☐	11:1—12:17 ☐	13:1-27 ☐	14:1-22 ☐	15:1-21 ☐	16:1—17:27 ☐	18:1-23 ☐
85	19:1—20:18 ☐	21:1—22:30 ☐	23:1-40 ☐	24:1—25:38 ☐	26:1—27:22 ☐	28:1—29:32 ☐	30:1-24 ☐
86	31:1-23 ☐	31:24-40 ☐	32:1-44 ☐	33:1-26 ☐	34:1-22 ☐	35:1-19 ☐	36:1-32 ☐
87	37:1-21 ☐	38:1-28 ☐	39:1—40:16 ☐	41:1—42:22 ☐	43:1—44:30 ☐	45:1—46:28 ☐	47:1—48:16 ☐
88	48:17-47 ☐	49:1-22 ☐	49:23-39 ☐	50:1-27 ☐	50:28-46 ☐	51:1-27 ☐	51:28-64 ☐
89	52:1-34 ☐	Lam. 1:1-22 ☐	2:1-22 ☐	3:1-39 ☐	3:40-66 ☐	4:1-22 ☐	5:1-22 ☐
90	Ezek. 1:1-14 ☐	1:15-28 ☐	2:1—3:27 ☐	4:1—5:17 ☐	6:1—7:27 ☐	8:1—9:11 ☐	10:1—11:25 ☐
91	12:1—13:23 ☐	14:1—15:8 ☐	16:1-63 ☐	17:1—18:32 ☐	19:1-14 ☐	20:1-49 ☐	21:1-32 ☐
92	22:1-31 ☐	23:1-49 ☐	24:1-27 ☐	25:1—26:21 ☐	27:1-36 ☐	28:1-26 ☐	29:1—30:26 ☐
93	31:1—32:32 ☐	33:1-33 ☐	34:1-31 ☐	35:1—36:21 ☐	36:22-38 ☐	37:1-28 ☐	38:1—39:29 ☐
94	40:1-27 ☐	40:28-49 ☐	41:1-26 ☐	42:1—43:27 ☐	44:1-31 ☐	45:1-25 ☐	46:1-24 ☐
95	47:1-23 ☐	48:1-35 ☐	Dan. 1:1-21 ☐	2:1-30 ☐	2:31-49 ☐	3:1-30 ☐	4:1-37 ☐
96	5:1-31 ☐	6:1-28 ☐	7:1-12 ☐	7:13-28 ☐	8:1-27 ☐	9:1-27 ☐	10:1-21 ☐
97	11:1-22 ☐	11:23-45 ☐	12:1-13 ☐	Hosea 1:1-11 ☐	2:1-23 ☐	3:1—4:19 ☐	5:1-15 ☐
98	6:1-11 ☐	7:1-16 ☐	8:1-14 ☐	9:1-17 ☐	10:1-15 ☐	11:1-12 ☐	12:1-14 ☐
99	13:1—14:9 ☐	Joel 1:1-20 ☐	2:1-16 ☐	2:17-32 ☐	3:1-21 ☐	Amos 1:1-15 ☐	2:1-16 ☐
100	3:1-15 ☐	4:1—5:27 ☐	6:1—7:17 ☐	8:1—9:15 ☐	Obad. 1-21 ☐	Jonah 1:1-17 ☐	2:1—4:11 ☐
101	Micah 1:1-16 ☐	2:1—3:12 ☐	4:1—5:15 ☐	6:1—7:20 ☐	Nahum 1:1-15 ☐	2:1—3:19 ☐	Hab. 1:1-17 ☐
102	2:1-20 ☐	3:1-19 ☐	Zeph. 1:1-18 ☐	2:1-15 ☐	3:1-20 ☐	Hag. 1:1-15 ☐	2:1-23 ☐
103	Zech. 1:1-21 ☐	2:1-13 ☐	3:1-10 ☐	4:1-14 ☐	5:1—6:15 ☐	7:1—8:23 ☐	9:1-17 ☐
104	10:1—11:17 ☐	12:1—13:9 ☐	14:1-21 ☐	Mal. 1:1-14 ☐	2:1-17 ☐	3:1-18 ☐	4:1-6 ☐

Reading Schedule for the Recovery Version of the New Testament with Footnotes

Wk.	Lord's Day	Monday	Tuesday	Wednesday	Thursday	Friday	Saturday
1	Matt. 1:1-2 ☐	1:3-7 ☐	1:8-17 ☐	1:18-25 ☐	2:1-23 ☐	3:1-6 ☐	3:7-17 ☐
2	4:1-11 ☐	4:12-25 ☐	5:1-4 ☐	5:5-12 ☐	5:13-20 ☐	5:21-26 ☐	5:27-48 ☐
3	6:1-8 ☐	6:9-18 ☐	6:19-34 ☐	7:1-12 ☐	7:13-29 ☐	8:1-13 ☐	8:14-22 ☐
4	8:23-34 ☐	9:1-13 ☐	9:14-17 ☐	9:18-34 ☐	9:35—10:5 ☐	10:6-25 ☐	10:26-42 ☐
5	11:1-15 ☐	11:16-30 ☐	12:1-14 ☐	12:15-32 ☐	12:33-42 ☐	12:43—13:2 ☐	13:3-12 ☐
6	13:13-30 ☐	13:31-43 ☐	13:44-58 ☐	14:1-13 ☐	14:14-21 ☐	14:22-36 ☐	15:1-20 ☐
7	15:21-31 ☐	15:32-39 ☐	16:1-12 ☐	16:13-20 ☐	16:21-28 ☐	17:1-13 ☐	17:14-27 ☐
8	18:1-14 ☐	18:15-22 ☐	18:23-35 ☐	19:1-15 ☐	19:16-30 ☐	20:1-16 ☐	20:17-34 ☐
9	21:1-11 ☐	21:12-22 ☐	21:23-32 ☐	21:33-46 ☐	22:1-22 ☐	22:23-33 ☐	22:34-46 ☐
10	23:1-12 ☐	23:13-39 ☐	24:1-14 ☐	24:15-31 ☐	24:32-51 ☐	25:1-13 ☐	25:14-30 ☐
11	25:31-46 ☐	26:1-16 ☐	26:17-35 ☐	26:36-46 ☐	26:47-64 ☐	26:65-75 ☐	27:1-26 ☐
12	27:27-44 ☐	27:45-56 ☐	27:57—28:15 ☐	28:16-20 ☐	Mark 1:1 ☐	1:2-6 ☐	1:7-13 ☐
13	1:14-28 ☐	1:29-45 ☐	2:1-12 ☐	2:13-28 ☐	3:1-19 ☐	3:20-35 ☐	4:1-25 ☐
14	4:26-41 ☐	5:1-20 ☐	5:21-43 ☐	6:1-29 ☐	6:30-56 ☐	7:1-23 ☐	7:24-37 ☐
15	8:1-26 ☐	8:27—9:1 ☐	9:2-29 ☐	9:30-50 ☐	10:1-16 ☐	10:17-34 ☐	10:35-52 ☐
16	11:1-16 ☐	11:17-33 ☐	12:1-27 ☐	12:28-44 ☐	13:1-13 ☐	13:14-37 ☐	14:1-26 ☐
17	14:27-52 ☐	14:53-72 ☐	15:1-15 ☐	15:16-47 ☐	16:1-8 ☐	16:9-20 ☐	Luke 1:1-4 ☐
18	1:5-25 ☐	1:26-46 ☐	1:47-56 ☐	1:57-80 ☐	2:1-8 ☐	2:9-20 ☐	2:21-39 ☐
19	2:40-52 ☐	3:1-20 ☐	3:21-38 ☐	4:1-13 ☐	4:14-30 ☐	4:31-44 ☐	5:1-26 ☐
20	5:27—6:16 ☐	6:17-38 ☐	6:39-49 ☐	7:1-17 ☐	7:18-23 ☐	7:24-35 ☐	7:36-50 ☐
21	8:1-15 ☐	8:16-25 ☐	8:26-39 ☐	8:40-56 ☐	9:1-17 ☐	9:18-26 ☐	9:27-36 ☐
22	9:37-50 ☐	9:51-62 ☐	10:1-11 ☐	10:12-24 ☐	10:25-37 ☐	10:38-42 ☐	11:1-13 ☐
23	11:14-26 ☐	11:27-36 ☐	11:37-54 ☐	12:1-12 ☐	12:13-21 ☐	12:22-34 ☐	12:35-48 ☐
24	12:49-59 ☐	13:1-9 ☐	13:10-17 ☐	13:18-30 ☐	13:31—14:6 ☐	14:7-14 ☐	14:15-24 ☐
25	14:25-35 ☐	15:1-10 ☐	15:11-21 ☐	15:22-32 ☐	16:1-13 ☐	16:14-22 ☐	16:23-31 ☐
26	17:1-19 ☐	17:20-37 ☐	18:1-14 ☐	18:15-30 ☐	18:31-43 ☐	19:1-10 ☐	19:11-27 ☐

Reading Schedule for the Recovery Version of the New Testament with Footnotes

Wk.	Lord's Day	Monday	Tuesday	Wednesday	Thursday	Friday	Saturday
27	Luke 19:28-48 ☐	20:1-19 ☐	20:20-38 ☐	20:39—21:4 ☐	21:5-27 ☐	21:28-38 ☐	22:1-20 ☐
28	22:21-38 ☐	22:39-54 ☐	22:55-71 ☐	23:1-43 ☐	23:44-56 ☐	24:1-12 ☐	24:13-35 ☐
29	24:36-53 ☐	John 1:1-13 ☐	1:14-18 ☐	1:19-34 ☐	1:35-51 ☐	2:1-11 ☐	2:12-22 ☐
30	2:23—3:13 ☐	3:14-21 ☐	3:22-36 ☐	4:1-14 ☐	4:15-26 ☐	4:27-42 ☐	4:43-54 ☐
31	5:1-16 ☐	5:17-30 ☐	5:31-47 ☐	6:1-15 ☐	6:16-31 ☐	6:32-51 ☐	6:52-71 ☐
32	7:1-9 ☐	7:10-24 ☐	7:25-36 ☐	7:37-52 ☐	7:53—8:11 ☐	8:12-27 ☐	8:28-44 ☐
33	8:45-59 ☐	9:1-13 ☐	9:14-34 ☐	9:35—10:9 ☐	10:10-30 ☐	10:31—11:4 ☐	11:5-22 ☐
34	11:23-40 ☐	11:41-57 ☐	12:1-11 ☐	12:12-24 ☐	12:25-36 ☐	12:37-50 ☐	13:1-11 ☐
35	13:12-30 ☐	13:31-38 ☐	14:1-6 ☐	14:7-20 ☐	14:21-31 ☐	15:1-11 ☐	15:12-27 ☐
36	16:1-15 ☐	16:16-33 ☐	17:1-5 ☐	17:6-13 ☐	17:14-24 ☐	17:25—18:11 ☐	18:12-27 ☐
37	18:28-40 ☐	19:1-16 ☐	19:17-30 ☐	19:31-42 ☐	20:1-13 ☐	20:14-18 ☐	20:19-22 ☐
38	20:23-31 ☐	21:1-14 ☐	21:15-22 ☐	21:23-25 ☐	Acts 1:1-8 ☐	1:9-14 ☐	1:15-26 ☐
39	2:1-13 ☐	2:14-21 ☐	2:22-36 ☐	2:37-41 ☐	2:42-47 ☐	3:1-18 ☐	3:19—4:22 ☐
40	4:23-37 ☐	5:1-16 ☐	5:17-32 ☐	5:33-42 ☐	6:1—7:1 ☐	7:2-29 ☐	7:30-60 ☐
41	8:1-13 ☐	8:14-25 ☐	8:26-40 ☐	9:1-19 ☐	9:20-43 ☐	10:1-16 ☐	10:17-33 ☐
42	10:34-48 ☐	11:1-18 ☐	11:19-30 ☐	12:1-25 ☐	13:1-12 ☐	13:13-43 ☐	13:44—14:5 ☐
43	14:6-28 ☐	15:1-12 ☐	15:13-34 ☐	15:35—16:5 ☐	16:6-18 ☐	16:19-40 ☐	17:1-18 ☐
44	17:19-34 ☐	18:1-17 ☐	18:18-28 ☐	19:1-20 ☐	19:21-41 ☐	20:1-12 ☐	20:13-38 ☐
45	21:1-14 ☐	21:15-26 ☐	21:27-40 ☐	22:1-21 ☐	22:22-29 ☐	22:30—23:11 ☐	23:12-15 ☐
46	23:16-30 ☐	23:31—24:21 ☐	24:22—25:5 ☐	25:6-27 ☐	26:1-13 ☐	26:14-32 ☐	27:1-26 ☐
47	27:27—28:10 ☐	28:11-22 ☐	28:23-31 ☐	Rom. 1:1-2 ☐	1:3-7 ☐	1:8-17 ☐	1:18-25 ☐
48	1:26—2:10 ☐	2:11-29 ☐	3:1-20 ☐	3:21-31 ☐	4:1-12 ☐	4:13-25 ☐	5:1-11 ☐
49	5:12-17 ☐	5:18—6:5 ☐	6:6-11 ☐	6:12-23 ☐	7:1-12 ☐	7:13-25 ☐	8:1-2 ☐
50	8:3-6 ☐	8:7-13 ☐	8:14-25 ☐	8:26-39 ☐	9:1-18 ☐	9:19—10:3 ☐	10:4-15 ☐
51	10:16—11:10 ☐	11:11-22 ☐	11:23-36 ☐	12:1-3 ☐	12:4-21 ☐	13:1-14 ☐	14:1-12 ☐
52	14:13-23 ☐	15:1-13 ☐	15:14-33 ☐	16:1-5 ☐	16:6-24 ☐	16:25-27 ☐	1 Cor. 1:1-4 ☐

Reading Schedule for the Recovery Version of the New Testament with Footnotes

Wk.	Lord's Day	Monday	Tuesday	Wednesday	Thursday	Friday	Saturday
53	1 Cor. 1:5-9	1:10-17	1:18-31	2:1-5	2:6-10	2:11-16	3:1-9
54	3:10-13	3:14-23	4:1-9	4:10-21	5:1-13	6:1-11	6:12-20
55	7:1-16	7:17-24	7:25-40	8:1-13	9:1-15	9:16-27	10:1-4
56	10:5-13	10:14-33	11:1-6	11:7-16	11:17-26	11:27-34	12:1-11
57	12:12-22	12:23-31	13:1-13	14:1-12	14:13-25	14:26-33	14:34-40
58	15:1-19	15:20-28	15:29-34	15:35-49	15:50-58	16:1-9	16:10-24
59	2 Cor. 1:1-4	1:5-14	1:15-22	1:23—2:11	2:12-17	3:1-6	3:7-11
60	3:12-18	4:1-6	4:7-12	4:13-18	5:1-8	5:9-15	5:16-21
61	6:1-13	6:14—7:4	7:5-16	8:1-15	8:16-24	9:1-15	10:1-6
62	10:7-18	11:1-15	11:16-33	12:1-10	12:11-21	13:1-10	13:11-14
63	Gal. 1:1-5	1:6-14	1:15-24	2:1-13	2:14-21	3:1-4	3:5-14
64	3:15-22	3:23-29	4:1-7	4:8-20	4:21-31	5:1-12	5:13-21
65	5:22-26	6:1-10	6:11-15	6:16-18	Eph. 1:1-3	1:4-6	1:7-10
66	1:11-14	1:15-18	1:19-23	2:1-5	2:6-10	2:11-14	2:15-18
67	2:19-22	3:1-7	3:8-13	3:14-18	3:19-21	4:1-4	4:5-10
68	4:11-16	4:17-24	4:25-32	5:1-10	5:11-21	5:22-26	5:27-33
69	6:1-9	6:10-14	6:15-18	6:19-24	Phil. 1:1-7	1:8-18	1:19-26
70	1:27—2:4	2:5-11	2:12-16	2:17-30	3:1-6	3:7-11	3:12-16
71	3:17-21	4:1-9	4:10-23	Col. 1:1-8	1:9-13	1:14-23	1:24-29
72	2:1-7	2:8-15	2:16-23	3:1-4	3:5-15	3:16-25	4:1-18
73	1 Thes. 1:1-3	1:4-10	2:1-12	2:13—3:5	3:6-13	4:1-10	4:11—5:11
74	5:12-28	2 Thes. 1:1-12	2:1-17	3:1-18	1 Tim. 1:1-2	1:3-4	1:5-14
75	1:15-20	2:1-7	2:8-15	3:1-13	3:14—4:5	4:6-16	5:1-25
76	6:1-10	6:11-21	2 Tim. 1:1-10	1:11-18	2:1-15	2:16-26	3:1-13
77	3:14—4:8	4:9-22	Titus 1:1-4	1:5-16	2:1-15	3:1-8	3:9-15
78	Philem. 1:1-11	1:12-25	Heb. 1:1-2	1:3-5	1:6-14	2:1-9	2:10-18

Reading Schedule for the Recovery Version of the New Testament with Footnotes

Wk.	Lord's Day	Monday	Tuesday	Wednesday	Thursday	Friday	Saturday
79	Heb. 3:1-6 □	3:7-19 □	4:1-9 □	4:10-13 □	4:14-16 □	5:1-10 □	5:11—6:3 □
80	6:4-8 □	6:9-20 □	7:1-10 □	7:11-28 □	8:1-6 □	8:7-13 □	9:1-4 □
81	9:5-14 □	9:15-28 □	10:1-18 □	10:19-28 □	10:29-39 □	11:1-6 □	11:7-19 □
82	11:20-31 □	11:32-40 □	12:1-2 □	12:3-13 □	12:14-17 □	12:18-26 □	12:27-29 □
83	13:1-7 □	13:8-12 □	13:13-15 □	13:16-25 □	James 1:1-8 □	1:9-18 □	1:19-27 □
84	2:1-13 □	2:14-26 □	3:1-18 □	4:1-10 □	4:11-17 □	5:1-12 □	5:13-20 □
85	1 Pet. 1:1-2 □	1:3-4 □	1:5 □	1:6-9 □	1:10-12 □	1:13-17 □	1:18-25 □
86	2:1-3 □	2:4-8 □	2:9-17 □	2:18-25 □	3:1-13 □	3:14-22 □	4:1-6 □
87	4:7-16 □	4:17-19 □	5:1-4 □	5:5-9 □	5:10-14 □	2 Pet. 1:1-2 □	1:3-4 □
88	1:5-8 □	1:9-11 □	1:12-18 □	1:19-21 □	2:1-3 □	2:4-11 □	2:12-22 □
89	3:1-6 □	3:7-9 □	3:10-12 □	3:13-15 □	3:16 □	3:17-18 □	1 John 1:1-2 □
90	1:3-4 □	1:5 □	1:6 □	1:7 □	1:8-10 □	2:1-2 □	2:3-11 □
91	2:12-14 □	2:15-19 □	2:20-23 □	2:24-27 □	2:28-29 □	3:1-5 □	3:6-10 □
92	3:11-18 □	3:19-24 □	4:1-6 □	4:7-11 □	4:12-15 □	4:16—5:3 □	5:4-13 □
93	5:14-17 □	5:18-21 □	2 John 1:1-3 □	1:4-9 □	1:10-13 □	3 John 1:1-6 □	1:7-14 □
94	Jude 1:1-4 □	1:5-10 □	1:11-19 □	1:20-25 □	Rev. 1:1-3 □	1:4-6 □	1:7-11 □
95	1:12-13 □	1:14-16 □	1:17-20 □	2:1-6 □	2:7 □	2:8-9 □	2:10-11 □
96	2:12-14 □	2:15-17 □	2:18-23 □	2:24-29 □	3:1-3 □	3:4-6 □	3:7-9 □
97	3:10-13 □	3:14-18 □	3:19-22 □	4:1-5 □	4:6-7 □	4:8-11 □	5:1-6 □
98	5:7-14 □	6:1-8 □	6:9-17 □	7:1-8 □	7:9-17 □	8:1-6 □	8:7-12 □
99	8:13—9:11 □	9:12-21 □	10:1-4 □	10:5-11 □	11:1-4 □	11:5-14 □	11:15-19 □
100	12:1-4 □	12:5-9 □	12:10-18 □	13:1-10 □	13:11-18 □	14:1-5 □	14:6-12 □
101	14:13-20 □	15:1-8 □	16:1-12 □	16:13-21 □	17:1-6 □	17:7-18 □	18:1-8 □
102	18:9—19:4 □	19:5-10 □	19:11-16 □	19:17-21 □	20:1-6 □	20:7-10 □	20:11-15 □
103	21:1 □	21:2 □	21:3-8 □	21:9-13 □	21:14-18 □	21:19-21 □	21:22-27 □
104	22:1 □	22:2 □	22:3-11 □	22:12-15 □	22:16-17 □	22:18-21 □	

Week 4 — Day 6 — Today's verses

Rom. Because those whom He foreknew, He
8:29-30 also predestinated *to be* conformed to the
image of His Son...; and those whom He
predestinated, these He also called; and
those whom He called, these He also justified; and those whom He justified, these
He also glorified.

Col. And have put on the new man, which is
3:10-11 being renewed unto full knowledge according to the image of Him who created
him, where...Christ is all and in all.

_____
Date

Week 4 — Day 5 — Today's verses

Rom. For if we, being enemies, were reconciled
5:10 to God through the death of His Son, much
more we will be saved in His life, having
been reconciled.

12:2 And do not be fashioned according to this
age, but be transformed by the renewing
of the mind that you may prove what the
will of God is...

5 So we who are many are one Body in
Christ, and individually members one of
another.

_____
Date

Week 4 — Day 4 — Today's verses

Heb. For it was fitting for Him,...in leading
2:10 many sons into glory, to make the Author
of their salvation perfect through suffer-
ings.

Rev. He who has an ear, let him hear what the
2:17 Spirit says to the churches. To him who
overcomes, to him I will give of the hidden manna, and to him I will give a white
stone, and upon the stone a new name
written, which no one knows except him
who receives *it.*

_____
Date

Week 4 — Day 3 — Today's verses

Heb. ...We have such a High Priest, who sat
8:1 down at the right hand of the throne of
the Majesty in the heavens.

7:25 Hence also He is able to save to the uttermost those who come forward to God
through Him, since He lives always to intercede for them.

Col. Persevere in prayer, watching in it with
4:2 thanksgiving.

_____
Date

Week 4 — Day 2 — Today's verses

Col. For you died, and your life is hidden with
3:3-4 Christ in God. When Christ our life is
manifested, then you also will be manifested with Him in glory.

_____
Date

Week 4 — Day 1 — Today's verses

Col. If therefore you were raised together with
3:1-2 Christ, seek the things which are above,
where Christ is, sitting at the right hand of
God. Set your mind on the things which
are above, not on the things which are on
the earth.

_____
Date

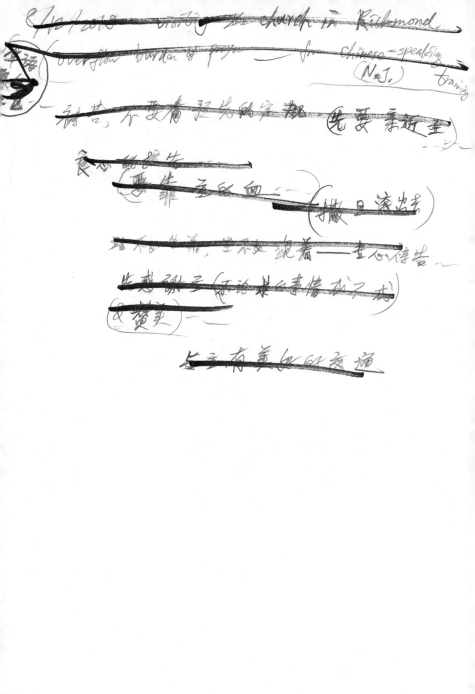

11/1/2018 visiting the church in Richmond
overflow burden of prayer for chinese-speaking
(N.J.) training

祷告, 个要有召 的宇期 (先要 亲近主)

愿意 妹愿生

要告 受成血 (撒日 滚出去)

话不的 话, 坐下来 靠着——主心得告

些亲孩子 (所流共爱情书了去)

& 赞美

左去有羡 的爱 顶

6/19 — Prayer

Italy — (pray for island of Malta) open to gospel

(Raymond — sick? now in Taiwan & (whole family
salvation —

Mission college — Wen-Hsing's contact Jose —

(6/17)⁶ 2-4pm   sisters' fellowship (by bro Minoru)
(sign up by 6/24)

(Video Training) will be in Cupertino meeting hall
(7/4, 7, 8, 14, 15)   (10081 Pasadena Ave)

(6/17 deadline for SST sign up   (Jorge, Wendsing, Arnold will go
(7/22 - 27)   Dan Ye, (7/5 ½), & Vicky

Hebrew
LS #25-26